WOODWORKING
The New Wave

Books by Dona Z. Meilach

WOODWORKING
CONTEMPORARY ART WITH WOOD
CREATING MODERN FURNITURE
CREATING SMALL WOOD OBJECTS AS FUNCTIONAL SCULPTURE

SCULPTURE
CONTEMPORARY STONE SCULPTURE
CREATING ART WITH BREAD DOUGH
CREATING WITH PLASTER
CREATIVE CARVING
DECORATIVE AND SCULPTURAL IRONWORK
DIRECT METAL SCULPTURE with Donald Seiden
SCULPTURE CASTING with Dennis Kowal

JEWELRY
ETHNIC JEWELRY

FIBERS AND FABRICS
BASKETRY TODAY WITH MATERIALS FROM NATURE with Dee Menagh
CONTEMPORARY BATIK AND TIE-DYE
CONTEMPORARY LEATHER
CREATING ART FROM FIBERS AND FABRICS
CREATIVE STITCHERY with Lee Erlin Snow
EXOTIC NEEDLEWORK WITH ETHNIC PATTERNS with Dee Menagh
MACRAMÉ ACCESSORIES
MACRAMÉ CREATIVE DESIGN IN KNOTTING
MACRAMÉ GNOMES AND PUPPETS
MAKING CONTEMPORARY RUGS AND WALL HANGINGS
A MODERN APPROACH TO BASKETRY WITH FIBERS AND GRASSES
PLANT HANGERS
SOFT SCULPTURE AND OTHER SOFT ART FORMS
WEAVING OFF-LTOM with Lee Erlin Snow

CERAMIC-TILE
TILE DECORATING WITH GEMMA

DESIGN
THE ARTIST'S EYE
HOW TO CREATE YOUR OWN DESIGNS with Jay and Bill Hinz

COLLAGE-PAPER
ACCENT ON CRAFTS
BOX ART: ASSEMBLAGE AND CONSTRUCTION
COLLAGE AND ASSEMBLAGE with Elvie Ten Hoor
CREATING ART FROM ANYTHING
PAPERCRAFT
PAPIER-MÂCHÉ ARTISTRY
PRINTMAKING

EXERCISE-HEALTH
THE ART OF BELLY-DANCING with Dahlena
JAZZERCISE with Judi Sheppard Missett
HOW TO RELIEVE YOUR ACHING BACK

COOKING
HOMEMADE LIQUEURS with Mel Meilach
MARINADE MAGIC

Dona Z. Meilach

WOODWORKING
The New Wave

Today's Design Trends in
Objects, Furniture and Sculpture
with Artist Interviews

CROWN PUBLISHERS, INC.
NEW YORK
Distributed outside the United States and Canada by Fleetbooks

It gives me great pleasure to dedicate this book to
Brandt Aymar, The Perfect Editor

Inquiries should be addressed to Crown Publishers, Inc.,
One Park Avenue, New York, New York 10016

Printed in the United States of America

Published simultaneously in Canada by General Publishing Company Limited

Distributed outside the United States and Canada by Fleetbooks,
100 Park Avenue, New York, New York 10017

Library of Congress Cataloging in Publication Data

Meilach, Dona Z.
    Woodworking: The new wave.

    Includes index.
    1. Woodwork. 2. Wood-carving. 3. Furniture making.   I. Title.
TT180.M384 684'.08 81-190   AACR2
ISBN: 0-517-541920 (cloth)
      0-517-544830 (paper)

Book design by Dona Z. Meilach

10 9 8 7 6 5 4 3 2 1

First Edition

Contents

Preface

The statements most often heard when I am gathering material for a book like this are: "You must have fun interviewing so many artists, seeing so many studios, visiting galleries. Can I help carry your cameras?"

Rather than turn down potential volunteers, let me share with you some aspects of assembling the materials. You may recognize the wisdom of sitting comfortably in your own studios and enjoying it all vicariously.

People contacted: artists, galleries, collectors, photographers, with correspondence involved back and forth many times	629
In-studio interviews and photography	104
Photographs submitted in black and white and color	2,422
Photographs used	624

There is no way to calculate time spent answering correspondence, the costs of secretarial help, mailing, my own photography and travel. The entire project from inception of idea to finished manuscript was twenty-two months. Another ten months was required for the publication process.

"Gathering" also included notices in magazines, which generated hundreds of inquiries. Of the 550 inquiries from artists, 345 of them submitted photographs. The work of 189 artists was used. There were attendance at and participation in woodworking conferences, visits to suppliers and to libraries. There were uncountable trips to the photo processor and scores of long-distance telephone calls to clear up sizes of finished pieces and types of wood and to secure better photographic prints and statements about the work.

Undoubtedly, the most frustrating aspect of writing an art book is the inordinate number of poor quality photographs submitted, a major reason for the rejection of a majority of pieces. Problems included impossible backgrounds, such as folded and wrinkled sheets, and patterned floors and wallpapers. Blurred, out-of-focus and poor depth-of-field photographs, wrong exposures, bad lighting and/or poor developing were too much in evidence. I feel strongly that a book devoted to an art form must be visually artistic itself.

Acknowledgments

I wish I could acknowledge individually all those who have in some way helped with this book. I want to thank all woodworkers everywhere who cooperated and sent in photographs. When I had to return them unused, it hurt me as much as it hurt you. I feel especially warm and "like family" when I recall all of you and your words of appreciation when I met you at conferences, schools, lectures and bookstores. It was those of you who prodded and encouraged me, during the first wookworking conference in Berkeley, California, in February 1979, who are responsible for my undertaking this compilation. I had gathered slides for the presentation, but I had no intention of tackling another major book until you and you and you told me how much my earlier books influenced your teaching and your work and even the development of wood as an art form.

I also want to thank the many gallery owners who suggested people for me to reach: Ron Isaacson and Deborah Farber-Isaacson of The Mindscape Gallery, Evanston, Illinois; Jan Francis of The Del Mano Gallery, Los Angeles; Inga W. Heck of The A. J. Wood Galleries, Philadelphia; Ruth and Rick Snyderman of The Works Gallery, Philadelphia, and B. J. Adams of The Art in Fiber Gallery, Washington, D.C.

I am also indebted to the following for their help: Debbie and Chris Ray of Philadelphia; Tom Tramel and Ralph Evans of California State University in Northridge; Lawrence B. Hunter of San Diego State University; Chuck Masters of San Diego, California; and Dean Santner of Emeryville, California.

My special gratitude goes to Collette Russell, who helped with correspondence and kept track of photographs submitted. And I cannot emphasize adequately the continuing support and patience of my husband, Dr. Mel Meilach, who *does* help drag cameras. I am sure there are times when he would gladly relinquish his allegedly "glamour job" to anyone crazy enough to volunteer.

I appreciate the freedom given to me by my editor, Brandt Aymar, to develop the format of the book, and thank his staff as well for bringing it all to fruition so beautifully.

DONA Z. MEILACH   CARLSBAD, CALIFORNIA 1981

Contributors

Adams, Peter Michael; North Carolina
Agate, Joseph A.; Illinois
Alexander, Richard; California
Allman, Pamela; Florida
Armijo, Federico; New Mexico
Ayers, Doug; California
Azoff, Mitchell; Wisconsin
Bailey, Phillip; California
Behl, Wolfgang; Connecticut
Belserene, Susan Gray; Canada
Bennett, Garry K.; California
Blunk J. B.; California
Boomer, John; New Mexico
Bourdon, Robert; Wyoming
Boyd, Jack; California
Briggs, Jeffrey A.; Massachusetts
Brooks, Jon; New Hampshire
Brown, Tom; California
Buchen, Bill; New York
Buchen, Mary; New York
Buchner, Saumitra Lewis; California
Carlin, David; California
Carroll, Dickson; Washington, D.C.
Casey, Stephen L.; California
Cataldo, Irene Gennaro; New York
Cave, Leonard C; Maryland
Chappelow, Bill; California
Clary, Morse; Washington
Cobb, Charles B.; California
Coffey, Michael; Vermont
Cooper, Michael; California
Cummings, Frank E.; California
Curtis, Timothy P.; Missouri
Dadey, Ed; Nebraska
Dasenbrock, Diedrich; Oregon
Deasy, Jerry; Illinois
Decker, Bruce; California
De Villiers, Jephan; Belgium
DeWit, Margo; Pennsylvania
Dieringer, Ken; Oregon
Dohany, Jack; California
Duncan, Tom; New York
Eaves, Winslow; New Hampshire
Egerton, Bridget; England

Egerton, Frank; England
Elgin, Lee; Colorado
Ellsworth, David; Colorado
Evans, William Jaquith; California
Ewing, Robert; California
Falwell, Bobby Reed; Kentucky
Feese, Richard; California
Ferrara, Jackie; New York
Fink, Jesse Roy; California
Flatt, David G.; Wisconsin
Fleck, Jan; Florida
Fogel, Jacqueline; New York
Fougner, Allan; California
Freerksen, Doug; Illinois
Friedman, Alan; New York
Galbraith, Gary; Washington
Garvey, Albert; California
Gilson, Giles; New York
Givotovsky, Igor; Massachusetts
Goldberg, Margery Eleme; District of
    Columbia
Goldfinger, Michael; Vermont
Gomez, Manuel A.; California
Goo, Ben; Arizona
Graham, Michael N.; California
Green, David L.; Washington
Gronborg, Erik; California
Gundry, Hugh; California
Guttin, Bruce; California
Halbom, William E.; Washington
Hampson, Nicholas; California
Hayles, Mona; California
Hazama, Karen; California
Hendrickson, Doug; Iowa
Herzog, Joanne; California
Herzog, Robert; California
Hoare, Tyler James; California
Hoffman, Joshua; New York
Hogbin, Stephen; Canada
Holzapfel, David; Vermont
Hopkins, Jack Rogers; California
Hoptner, Richard; Pennsylvania
Horgos, Bill; California
Hunter, Lawrence B.; California

Hutchinson, Mabel B.; California
Irvin, Kevin M.; Indiana
Isaacs, Ron; Kentucky
Jaffe, Sara; California
Johnson, Carl E.; California
Johnson, C. R.; Wisconsin
Johnson, Ralph; California
Kaplan, Charles M.; Illinois
Kaplan, Jon; New Mexico
Kaplowitz, Caroline Gassner; New York
Karrol, Reuben H.; New Jersey
Kelley, C. Regina; Maine
Kent, Ron; Hawaii
Keyser, Bill; New York
King, David; California
King, Sterling; California
Kovacs, Craig M.; California
Kowalewski, John; California
Laske, Lyle; Minnesota
LePage, Bruce; Wisconsin
Levin, Mark S.; Illinois
Lindquist, Mark; New Hampshire
Livingston, William H.; California
Loar, Steve; Illinois
Longhurst, Bob; New York
Lowe, Douglas; California
Madsen, Steve; New Mexico
Magruder, R. Clark; Texas
Maiwald, Kathleen; California
Makepeace, John; England
Malloff, Georganna Pearce; Canada
Marc, Anton; New York
March, Robert E.; Massachusetts
Mason, Robert D.; California
Masters, Chuck; California
McCaffrey, Jeffrey T.; Wisconsin
McDermott, Lauren; New York
McNaughton, John W.; Indiana
Moore, Ronald S.; California
Mordaunt, Mel; California
Morinaka, Dennis; California
Musia, Amy; Indiana
Newhall, Mike; Wisconsin
Norhausen, Heinz; California
Pagh, Ejner C.; Illinois
Patrick, William; Vermont
Paulsen, Stephen M.; California
Pearce, Michael; California
Perrone, Bobb; Vermont
Pohlers, Rick; California
Presslor, William L.; Indiana

Quinn, Saswathan; California
Rannefeld, James; New Mexico
Rauschke, Tom; Wisconsin
Richardson, William M.; California
Rising, Martha; California
Robbie, Peter; New Hampshire
Rogers, Ronnie J.; Texas
Ruhlman, Paul; Massachusetts
Runge, Paul; Texas
Sabo, Irving; Connecticut
Sabosik, George A.; Wisconsin
Sakwa, Hap; California
Santner, Dean; California
Schmutzhart, Berthold J.; District of
  Columbia
Schule, Don; Texas
Schwab, Terry; Wisconsin
Scott, Robert W.; Wisconsin
Sellew, Dick; California
Siegel, Alan; New York
Smullin, Frank; North Carolina
Snyder, Hills; Texas
Splane, Robson Lindsay, Jr.; California
Spring, Barbara; California
Stegeman, Dr. Arthur L.; California
Stevens, Michael K.; California
Sylvester, Gary; California
Talarico, Sam; Pennsylvania
Taylor, Gib; Vermont
Teller, Jane; New Jersey
Tickel, William; Colorado
Trotman, Bob; North Carolina
VanLear, Robin; California
Vega, Ed; New Mexico
Voorheis, Steve; Montana
Wall, Fred; Virginia
Wall, John; Vermont
Wallace, Jim; Tennessee
Way, Lynn; California
Werner, Howard; New York
Wesler, Hugh; Wisconsin
Whitley, Robert C.; Pennsylvania
Widett, Neal M.; Massachusetts
Widstrand, Kurt; California
Wiken, Kaaren; Wisconsin
Wildnauer, Fred; Illinois
Willner, Andrew J.; Pennsylvania
Wilson, Susan Chandler; Massachusetts
Yaruss, Daniel; California
Yoshimura, Fumio; New York
Zimmerman, Walt; California

NOTE: To anyone who wishes to contact a specific artist about commissions or exhibitions: Direct your inquiry to the author in care of Crown Publishers, Inc., One Park Avenue, New York, New York 10016. Please include necessary forwarding postage or stamped self-addressed envelopes.

Introduction—Riding "The New Wave"

A book, like a sculpture, is a creative endeavor. Its creation parallels the processes that each artist brings to his materials. Originally, I envisioned a book that would encompass many facets of woodworking: finished pieces, discussions with people who were making them, philosophies, problems, tools, approaches to selling, publicity, becoming known and not becoming known—the frustrations and the successes.

During the early research, I sensed my raw material leading in a direction of its own like the grain in a piece of wood, the check in a log. Such is the nature of any creative work. I scrutinized the material I had to work with, then I sought out supplementary angles I might explore.

My direction was further dictated by my tastes and ideas. As I evaluated what I saw, I reestablished my premises. First, I would concentrate on exploring new directions for wood in art. Much of the work, I observed, was from well-established artists who had already reevaluated their expressive angles and experiences and sought channels of new discovery. Their recent work, much of which had not been seen by the public, represented both timid and tumultuous approaches. Among these artists were teachers who had presented a potential new range of visual imagery to their students. An entire new wave was beginning to swell. Many of these students were becoming professionals, lustily swimming about in a fertile milieu.

It was this energy that I wanted to capture in the work that was to involve and absorb my enthusiasm for nearly two years, from the earliest glimmer of the idea until the manuscript was delivered to the publisher.

Another aspect of the premise was to depict similarities and solutions to creative problems, approaches, techniques and equipment, whether the finished piece was functional or nonfunctional. I am impatient and bored with the age-old clichés and dead-end arguments, such as What is art? What is craft? And the differences between "fine arts" and "useful arts." One sculptor argued that the words "functional sculpture" were impossible to combine. I stifled a yawn and accused him of having an elitist attitude. A toymaker, whose toys are marvelously sculptural, suggested that "artists" have "studios" and "woodworkers" have "shops."

I am annoyed with the juggling of nonsensical semantic nuances. Regardless of whether any of the pieces illustrated has an obvious use or exists as intellectual stimulation (or functional versus nonfunctional, if you prefer), the artist's creative processes are the same: visualization, execution, results, audience. Whether a sinuous form is the leg of a chair or a soaring phallic symbol, the artist has to cope with the same problems, use the same tools, give attention to scale, space, form and finish. And he needs an audience, one that will appreciate his work whether it is to be played with, smiled at, sat upon or placed on a pedestal and viewed.

I won't suggest that I will solve this ever-present dichotomy between art-craft and artist-craftsman. If I can remove one small portion of the hyphen that separates them, I will have accomplished something for those who follow after me. Perhaps the selected examples will emphasize the quality of work needed to bury the argument completely.

Once premises were defined, I sought photographs, work to be photographed and people to be interviewed. I was concerned mainly with results, not a person's prior reputation, experience or publicity. Examples from a well-known woodworker may be next to those of a student. I sought pieces that showed energy, enthusiasm, ideas and respect for the medium. Then began the massive job of selecting, rejecting, laying out, sizing photographs, writing, revising, adding, deleting, sanding and polishing.

I do not mean to deny the existence of beautiful traditional furniture or to ignore those who create it. All have my utmost admiration. I appreciate the toil, sweat and hope expended on every piece of wood that is handled and shaped. Traditionalists have already accused me of discriminating against them in favor of the new and novel, but weren't Chippendale, Queen Anne and art nouveau once new and novel too? For the purpose of this book, their accusations are justified. "Traditional" has been around a long time; examples are available in profusion in books, shelter and architectural magazines. Only nuances in the changes are there to report. My intention was to explore new territory, not to travel over well-covered ground.

I submit that I am, possibly, the only one chronicling this new statement with no prejudices about who is making it. Nor am I concerned with the recently posed competition of West Coast versus East Coast activity.

This book is perhaps a personal statement, too, based on the many years I have been involved in the arts as an art historian and one who has published three previous books about woodworking and more than forty books covering trends and media of contemporary arts and crafts.

I sought the opinions of several consultants who work only in wood. I value their taste, knowledge of contemporary woodwork and ability to recognize excellent craftsmanship. Their role was to select their choices from the photographs available without knowing which examples others had chosen. Some agreed completely on many, disagreed on others. Where they were unanimous in selecting and rejecting, I invariably agreed with them. Additionally, they were able to recognize pieces so directly influenced by others that they bordered on "copying" without having sufficient integrity to warrant inclusion. Some examples, though influenced by previous trends, are valid because they represent a further step in a creative direction. The final selection is essentially mine within the physical limits of layout, number of pages, photograph sizes and other graphic considerations of a book.

My thanks to all of you who understand the thought and the incalculable hours of work involved, and who use and view my creative efforts.

COVER: McCALLISTER BOX—UNTITLED. Michael N. Graham.
Photograph, Robert Howell (see page 7 and color section)

PART I
OBJECTS

1

Containers

S mall containers to hold precious objects are themselves precious objects when they are works of art. Wood jewelry boxes, created by fine craftsmen for centuries, can be found in the history of many ancient and primitive cultures. They exhibit fine carving, detailed inlays and exquisite finishes. Their surfaces and interiors incorporate a wide range of sophisticated woodworking techniques.

Containers, made to hold any variety of precious or mundane objects, achieved artistic heights in societies where the need and tradition were established. Snuff boxes were fashioned by skilled craftsmen of Switzerland, France, Scotland, England, Russia and other countries where "sniffing" was popular. Now that "sniffing" is outmoded, the boxes have become highly prized collector's items.

The inro, the compartmented box worn on the sash of a Japanese kimono, was used as a toggle. Each compartment opened by sliding up and down on a string. When closed, the sections nestled neatly together. The entire piece was treated as one surface, intricately carved or painted to represent some private symbolism of the wearer. Some inro were made of lacquered wood, others of carved ivory, bone and varied materials. All are highly sought antiques today.

The contemporary container is a "collectible" item even while its use is in vogue. It may be collected because it is extraordinary or because the person who made it has an established reputation; its usefulness is not a factor. The container then has become an object. The maker may or may not use it as a point of departure for exploring form in the beautiful woods available to him.

Several artists interviewed explained that they were simply intrigued by the "container" and the potential for form within that definition. Michael N. Graham's wall form "Pipe Containers" represents a dynamic departure from the conventional box. Gone are the anticipated and comfortable square or rectangular shapes with flat sides. These are free-form pieces that appear to undulate, flow and hang; their surfaces are beautifully articulated, tactile and inviting.

The traditional round wooden box, whether hand carved or lathe turned, is emerging anew, also as a result of its encounter with the ideas of the times. The form may be altered, modified, fragmented and exploded into multitudinous

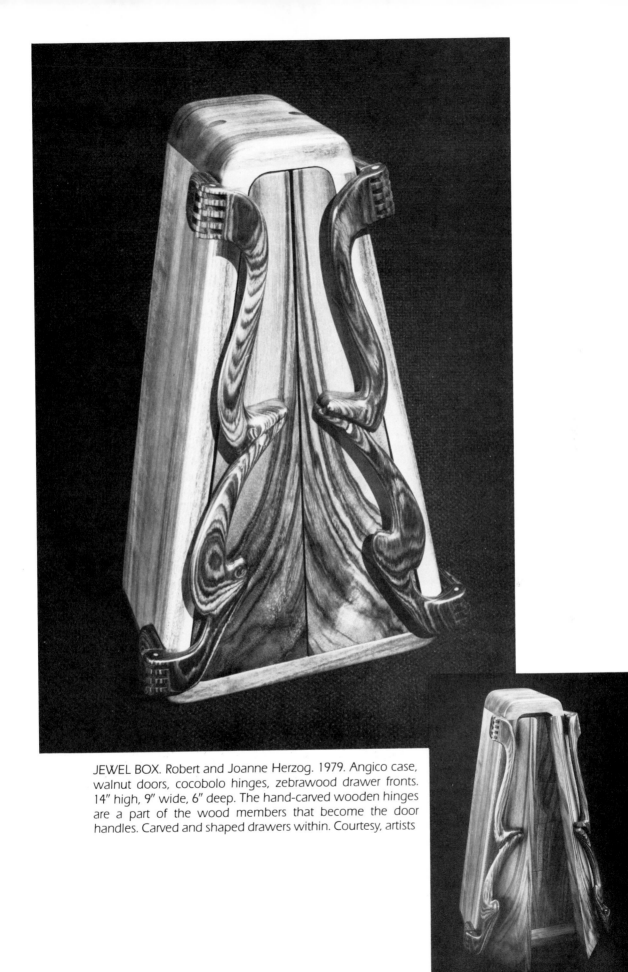

JEWEL BOX. Robert and Joanne Herzog. 1979. Angico case, walnut doors, cocobolo hinges, zebrawood drawer fronts. 14" high, 9" wide, 6" deep. The hand-carved wooden hinges are a part of the wood members that become the door handles. Carved and shaped drawers within. Courtesy, artists

JOURNEY TO A STRANGE LAND. Steve Madsen. Maple, ebony, tulipwood, vermilion, zebrawood, with ivory and silver. 10" high, 16" wide, 7" deep. Photograph, Jim Kraft

shapes and combinations of materials, and into bowls and bottles. Sides may have negative spaces that can make a bowl or bottle or box completely nonfunctional, but the suggestion of the original shape persists.

Mixed techniques, such as inlay, marquetry, assemblage and pyrography, are evident among the imaginative creative containers shown. Craftsmanship is no longer a problem; most of those who have become fascinated by their art are accomplished with joinery, carving and so forth. They play their tools much as does the accomplished musician at the piano.

Where will it all lead? The outlook is promising. For example, when Dean Santner made one-of-a-kind boxes, their acceptance was almost instant. He was incredulous and delighted. From his original boxes he refined the shapes and developed a line of craft multiples. Today, Santner's signed boxes appear in fine shops throughout the country and each is as carefully made as the original, though they now are completed with the aid of production procedures.

The marketplace has become brighter for the handmade crafted item. Whether one, ten, twenty, or a thousand items are made, a growing number of

OVALS, WINGS AND FEET. A lidded container. Giles Gilson. Walnut, cherry, apricot, rosewood. 7" high, 10¼" wide, 6½" deep. Photograph, Rick Siciliano

people are fascinated by and appreciative of them. A collector may even follow the development of a craftsman whose work he admires, and collect his pieces. The acceptance is a boost to the ego of the individual and to the entire art market as buyers become aware of individuals and cultivate them and their work.

Some of the containers are so frankly sculptured that it is not surprising to learn that the people who make them have been trained as sculptors or as artists in other media. There are also people who have had no formal art training. It is no surprise either that many of the artists whose names accompany the boxes, bottles and bowls in this chapter also are represented by sculpture and furniture.

Whether a form and its elements are assembled with traditional wood joinery, carved from a block of wood or from a log, turned on a lathe, hand-tool—gouged or developed with a chain saw or band saw is not important. The result must speak for itself. It must express the artist's thoughts, his originality, his ability to create a pleasing object. His touch is as individualistic as his signature at the bottom of a letter. What the object is made to contain is not so important so long as it is original, beautiful and beautifully made.

Michael Graham explains; "I simply wanted a drawer that curved." Regarding the radial drawer: "A true radiused section is first cut out of a piece of wood. The part that is left over acts as the housing which then receives a top and a bottom. The radiused section itself is the drawer which is hollowed out and fits the housing."

McCALLISTER BOX, GATE VALVE PIPE FORM. Michael N. Graham. 1980. Walnut, East Indian rosewood. 8" high, 11" wide, 28" deep.

BELOW: The Gate Valve Pipe Form container, open.

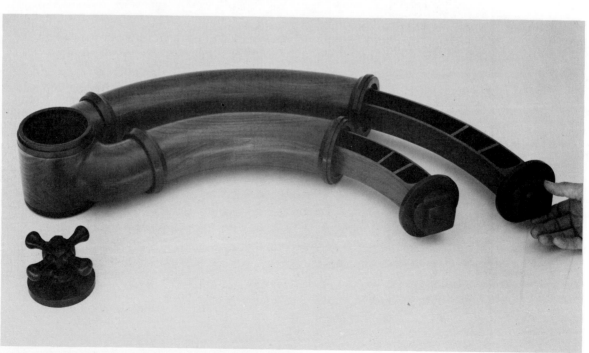

McCALLISTER BOX—UNTITLED.
Michael N. Graham. 1980. Padouk, East
Indian rosewood, walnut, imbuia,
bubinga. 10″ high, 10″ wide, 8″ deep.
Closed view. (See color insert and cover
for open view.)

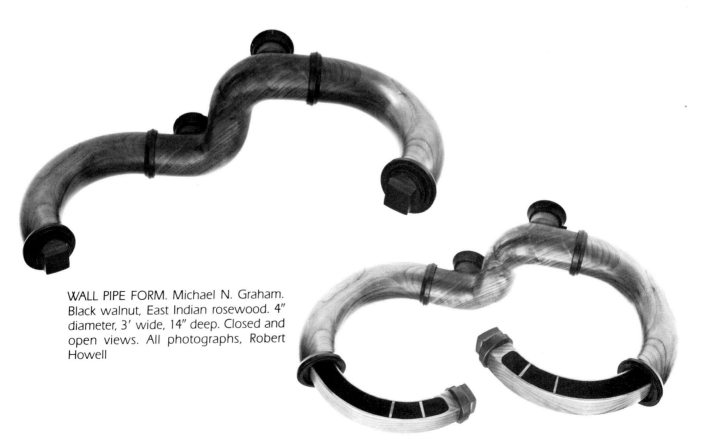

WALL PIPE FORM. Michael N. Graham.
Black walnut, East Indian rosewood. 4″
diameter, 3′ wide, 14″ deep. Closed and
open views. All photographs, Robert
Howell

7

TOP: CLOUD BOX WITH DRAWERS. Mark Lindquist. 1979.
Spalted maple. 8" high, 12" wide, 5" deep. Courtesy, artist

CLOUD BOX, lidded container. Mark Lindquist. 1979. 6" high,
12" wide, 6" deep. Courtesy, artist

8

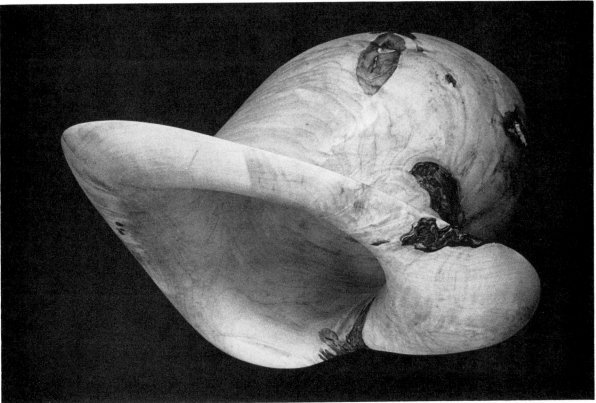

TOP: UNTITLED. Howard Werner. 1979. Sycamore. 10" high, 24" wide, 10" deep. Carved with chain saw and a ball mill on an air-powered die grinder.

UNTITLED. Howard Werner. 1980. Spalted maple. 2½" high, 2' wide, 2' deep. The forms, originally derived from functional turned bowls, are now developed as nonfunctional sculptures. Courtesy, artist.

BOWL. Hap Sakwa. 1980. Walnut. 5"
high, 10" diameter. Lathe turned, oil
finish.

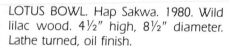

LOTUS BOWL. Hap Sakwa. 1980. Wild
lilac wood. 4½" high, 8½" diameter.
Lathe turned, oil finish.

LOTUS BOWL. Hap Sakwa. 1980. Wild
lilac wood. 4½" high, 8½" diameter.
Lathe turned, oil finish. All photographs,
artist

CONTAINER. David Ellsworth. Manzanita burl. 6½" high, 6½" deep.

CONTAINER. David Ellsworth. 1980. Desert ironwood. 6¼" high, 6¼" diameter. Photographs, artist

LAPPING WAVELET BOWL. Mark Lindquist. Elm burl. Turned and carved. 8" high. Collection, Metropolitan Museum of Art, New York. Courtesy, artist

EGG FORM BOWL. William Patrick. 1980. Spalted maple. 6"
high, 5" diameter. Lathe turned to ¼" thickness.

FLOWER FORM. William Patrick. 1980. Walnut. 5" high, 11"
diameter. Lathe turned to ¼" thickness. Courtesy, artist

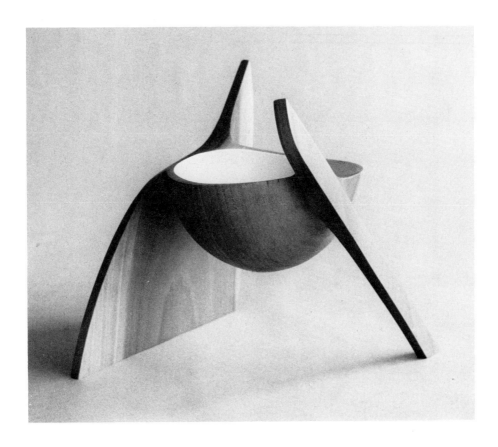

BOWLS. Stephen Hogbin. 1980. Poplar.

ABOVE: #435. 8½" high, 8" wide, 8" deep.
BELOW, LEFT: #432. 9½" high, 8¼" wide, 7¼" deep.
BELOW, RIGHT: #433. 8" high, 10¼" wide, 8¼" deep.
Photographs, J. James and Daughters

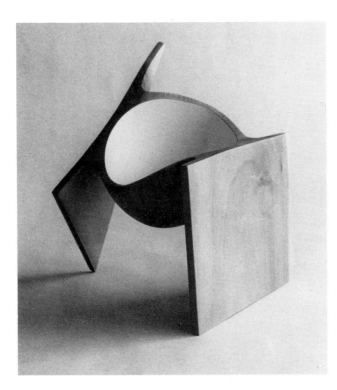

#2 HEAVY ARTILLERY. From the series "A Lady's Arsenal." William L. Presslor. 1980. Walnut, coffeenut, padouk, cherry, mahogany and aluminum. Lathe turned and laminated. Each piece is 13½" high, 4" diameter. Courtesy, artist
ABOVE: open view.

BANANA HEART BOX. Open and closed views. Ronnie J. Rogers. 1980. Cherry, maple and sassafras. Red satin pillow. Closed, 4¾" high, 13" wide, 16" deep. Movement is incorporated into the piece: When the lid is opened, a wire is activated that allows the banana shape to extend. Courtesy, artist

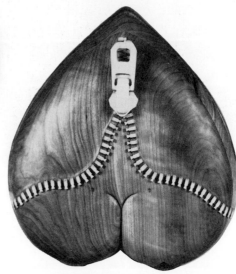

WOOD BOXES WITH CLOISONNÉ. Karen Hazama. 1979. Cherry, walnut and padouk. The tallest box is 12". All photographs, Dona Meilach

TINY BOXES. Karen Hazama. LEFT: Walnut box. FRONT: Ebony and silver box. 2½" wide, 1¾" deep. RIGHT: Turned Box. Cherry, walnut, padouk. 3½" diameter. Collection, Carol and Ralph Evans, Canoga Park, CA

JEWELRY BOX. Karen Hazama. Walnut, silver and enamel cloisonné, velvet. 5" high, 12" long, 8" wide. The central panel lifts off to unlock the lids, which swing out and reveal the four velvet-lined compartments.

BOX. Chuck Masters. 1980. Oak with formed leather top. 2" high, 4½" square. Courtesy, artist

FOUR-DRAWER JEWELRY BOX. David G. Flatt. Koa wood. 11½" high, 4" wide, 4" deep.

TWO-DRAWER JEWELRY BOX. David G. Flatt. Zebrawood. 9" high, 3½" wide, 4" deep. Courtesy, artist

SUSPENDED BOX. Dr. Arthur L. Stegeman. 1979. Myrtle wood. 7" high, 6¾" wide, 7½" deep. Courtesy, artist

EGG BOXES. Dean Santner. Koa wood. The larger box is 3¾" high, 14" long, 8" deep. The smaller box is made from the wood that remained within the drawer so as to utilize as much of the wood as possible. Courtesy, artist

HEART BOX. Dean Santner. Koa wood. Velour lined. Closed and open views. 3" high 8" wide, 6" deep. Santner's boxes are of high-quality machine-cut laminated-block construction. They are craft multiples. Courtesy, artist

CONTAINER. Mel Mordaunt. 1977. Walnut, East Indian rosewood and a "mystery white wood salvaged from a motorcycle crate." 4" high, 7" diameter. Courtesy, artist

Fantasy boxes with multiple compartments and wild, wonderful things going on within. All are carved from and into tree limbs.

GILLEY'S CASTLE. Tom Rauschke (wood) and Kaaren Wiken (fiber). Black walnut, maple, osage orange, with needlework. 19" high.

CHERRY TREEHOUSE. Tom Rauschke (wood) and Kaaren Wiken (fiber). Cherry, maple, plum, rosewood, electric light and fiber. 12" high.

THE DENTAL CHAIR. Tom Rauschke (wood) and Mike Newhall (scrimshaw inset). Black walnut, jarrah, tooth with scrimshaw. 12" high. The chair actually operates as does a real dental unit; it tips back and swivels, raises and lowers. The bottom "tooth" container portion is hinged so it opens and closes.

O'TANNENBAUM MUSIC BOX. Tom Rauschke (wood) and Kaaren Wiken (fiber). Russian olive, black walnut, rosewood; music box and fiber. 14" high. All photographs, artists

VOICE RESONANT BOWLS. John Boomer. 1980. Walnut. 4" high, 7" wide, 5" deep. Photograph, Peter L. Bloomer

BOTTLE. Ben Goo. Cherry and English leather, with brass escutcheon pins. Lathe turned. 5" high, 8½" diameter. Courtesy, artist

THE FUTURE OF THE WORLD IS IN
EGGS. Giles Gilson. A container of walnut. 13″ high, 12½″ diameter. Photograph, Rick Siciliano

FACE BOX. Bob Trotman. 1978. Ma-
hogany, walnut, dogwood, with in-
lay of acrylic resin star. 8½″ diameter.
Observe the hand-carved hinge.
Collection, Vice-President's House,
Washington, D.C. Photographs, Paul
Lemmons

FACE BOX. Bob Trotman, 1980. Walnut,
maple, mahogany, epoxy resin. 8½″
diameter. The stars are carved into the
wood, then filled in with epoxy resin
and smoothed down to the wood surface to yield the effect of inlay.

BOTTLES. Hand shaped. Stephen M. Paulsen. 1979–1980. The hand-shaped bottles are made of a variety of woods. Stoppers are lathe-turned. Glass vials are within. The tallest is 4" high. Courtesy, artist

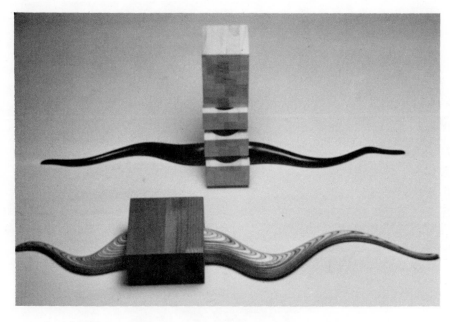

PARMA BOXES. Dean Santner. TOP: Pine and black enamel. 14" high, 30" wide. BOTTOM: Redwood box, with birch and spruce plies for extensions. 4" high, 32" wide. Courtesy, artist

JEWELRY BOX. Paul Ruhlman. 1978. Rock maple burl. 26″ high, 12″ diameter. Closed and open. Courtesy, artist

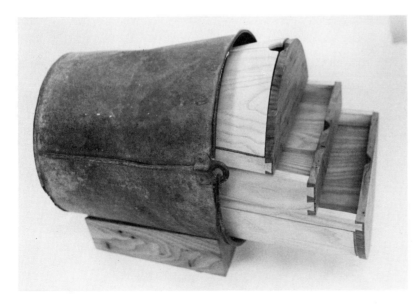

PAIL CABINET. Lauren McDermott. The imaginative result of a class assignment employing a found object. Photograph, Sally K. Davidson

BOTTLE. Stephen M. Paulsen. 1980. Ceonothus burl with turned and carved stopper and stand of Indian rosewood. Carved mask and draw pins. Removable glass vial within. Courtesy, artist

NESTED BOWLS. Two views. David Holzapfel. 1980. Eastern hop hornbeam burl. The largest bowl is 3" high, 13" diameter. Photograph, W. Allan Gill

PLATTER. Steve Loar. 1978. Maple and Padouk. 2¼" high, 14½" diameter. Lathe-turned platter with hand-carved alteration to achieve sculptured edge. Courtesy, artist

LAZY SUSAN WITH A NOSE FOR ART. Michael Pearce. Walnut, zebrawood, rosewood. 4½" high, 30" diameter. The top revolves on the base. Courtesy, artist

SERVING TRAY. Ben Goo. Walnut. 1" high, 22" wide, 14" deep. The raised cutting area is a natural rough finish to minimize cutting marks when used for cheese or meats. When the piece is not used as a tray, it is designed to be hung as a sculpture. Courtesy, artist

2

Functional Items

It would be challenging, exciting and never-ending to chronicle the variety of items made of wood by peoples throughout the world since man realized the potential of the material. In each time period, each culture, woodworkers made new items to serve specific needs, or fashioned already functional items in new ways. The comb is an example. It is an object of incredible delicacy and beauty in the coiffure of a Japanese geisha. A wooden comb used by African cultures has a completely different weight and sense of carving—not as delicate as the Japanese comb, but as serviceable.

When objects become obsolete, they may be replaced by more serviceable materials or altered usage. If a functional wooden item tends to deteriorate from time and use, another material may replace it: that's the nature of the system.

We have seen it happen in our own recent history. I find it fascinating to observe old wooden potato mashers, vegetable shredders, apple corers and butter churners appearing as decorative items in contemporary homes. It is chic to display an oxen yoke or a scythe handle on a wall. People have begun to appreciate the inherent beauty in such everyday objects—the wood used, the shapes and the patinas acquired from weathering and handling. The anonymous craftsmen of the past who whittled and sanded, spoke-shaved and planed, are gone. But many of the items they made are now in museums or treasured as collectibles for whatever nostalgic images they evoke.

The modern woodworker who creates avant-garde one-of-a-kind functional objects was not so long ago considered an anachronism. Perplexed people would wonder why anyone would bother to create something useful that could be made with less time and effort by machinery and purchased for less money.

Fortunately, thousands of people rebelled against the machine age and kept alive their taste for the hand-crafted object. It is fortunate, too, that there were those who continued to make such items and to keep their skills alive and their ideas fertile, as though oblivious to the plastics revolution.

These are people who love wood, who love to create, who find challenges in designing and hand-crafting mirrors, trays, scales, combs, toys, pipes, jewelry, cutting boards, platters and whatever stimulates their own visual fantasies.

26

CRYSTAL. Jeffrey Briggs. 1979. A wall mirror. The figure is carved from poplar. The hair and mirror rim are of Honduras mahogany. 31" high, 23" wide. The mirror is 13" diameter. Photograph, John I. Russell

FREE-STANDING MIRROR. Lee Elgin. Laminated cherry, luan, satinwood, vermilion and walnut. 78" high, 43" wide. Collection, Mr. J. D. Ackerman, Colorado Springs, CO

Each person brings to his art a variety of techniques. Many of their tools were unavailable to woodworkers of the past, yet some still prefer to use only mallet-driven gouges, slowly watching the shapes they envision emerge from a log or a board. Others may assemble, or lathe-turn, an object using the most efficient means they can find for the job. "It's what you make, not how you arrive at the results," said one toy maker. Still others investigate an assortment of techniques and use them as a vocabulary of woodworking. They combine materials, add and subtract wood at will.

The examples that follow illustrate many applications for creativity: veneering, pyrography, etching, marquetry and combinations of techniques. The results can be stunning, whether the woods are used alone or combined with metals, ivory, gold and silver.

The objects are offered to inspire the reader to develop his own technical vocabulary, resources and experiences.

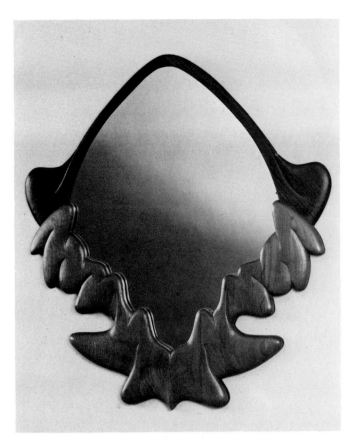

BURL MIRROR. Sam Talarico. 1974. Red Oak. 26" high, 30" wide. Courtesy, artist

MIRROR. Lee Elgin. Teak and walnut. 48" high, 44" wide. Collection, Mr. J. F. Connor, Denver, CO

CASSANDRA. Jeffrey Briggs. 1980. The figure is poplar, the hair is Honduras mahogany. Three laminations, carved. Rimless beveled topaz-tinted mirror. Overall size, 21" high, 31" wide. Photograph, Jack Russell

29

ARCHED WALL MIRROR. Steve Loar. 1979. Red oak and zebrawood. 32" high, 25" wide, 2" deep. Courtesy, artist

BELOW, LEFT: SMALL WALL MIRROR. Diedrich Dasenbrock. 1978. Alder, desert ironwood, glass. 9" high, 6" wide. 1" deep. Courtesy, artist

BELOW, RIGHT: MIRRORS. Mark S. Levin. Cherry and padouk. Each piece 72" high, 23" wide, 2" deep. Courtesy, artist

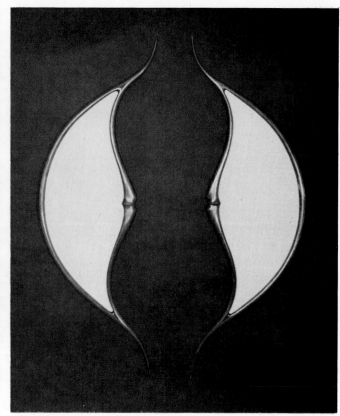

WALL MIRROR. Mitchell Azoff. Cherry and padouk. Steam bent. 15" high, 24" high. Photograph, William Lemke

MIRROR OR WINDOW. William E. Halbom. 1979. Stained pine. Figure carved front and back so it may be used as a free-hanging stained-glass window or as a two-sided mirror. 12" diameter. Photograph, Zoltan Gaal, Jr.

MIRRORS. Mona Hayles. 1978. Black walnut. 48" high, 52" wide. Courtesy, artist

HAND MIRROR. Frank E. Cummings.
1979. Ebony, ivory, zebra fur, 14K gold
and crystal. 17" high, 8½" wide.

WALL MIRROR. Frank E. Cummings.
Kingwood, Japanese pheasant feathers,
javalina feathers, leopard skin. 41" high,
18" wide. Photographs, Dona Meilach

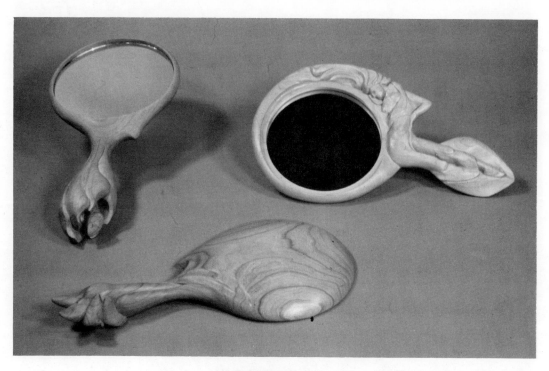

HAND MIRRORS. Jeffrey Briggs. 1978. The lady is rock maple,
the flower is brown oak, the bud is maple. Mirror, 6½"
diameter. Courtesy, artist

COMBS. Manuel A. Gomez. Varied exotic woods laminated and handcarved. Sizes approximately 10 to 12" high, 6" wide.

AKUA. Frank E. Cummings. African ebony, ivory, 14K gold, Icelandic wool. 11" high, 3½" wide.

HAND COMB. Frank E. Cummings. Ebony, ivory, 14K gold, jade. 10" long, 2" wide. Photographs, Dona Meilach

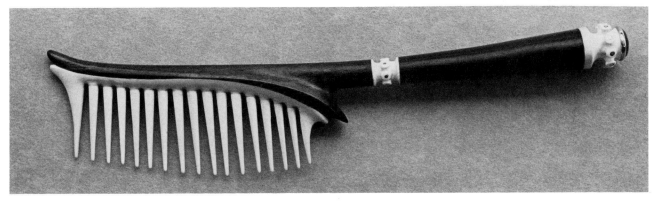

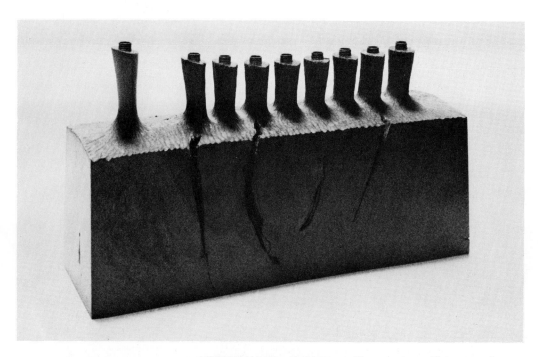

MENORAH. Chuck Masters. Claro walnut. 9″ high, 15″ long, 5″ deep. Courtesy, artist

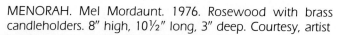

MENORAH. Mel Mordaunt. 1976. Rosewood with brass candleholders. 8″ high, 10½″ long, 3″ deep. Courtesy, artist

UTENSILS. Bill Chappelow. 1980. Assorted functional kitchen items hand carved and sculptured from a variety of woods including cherry, English walnut, black walnut, white oak.

Often the wood determines the shape of the object. Some of the wood is traded with other woodworkers; about one-third is purchased commercially, and the remainder is gleaned from the artist's own log pile. Photograph, Dona Meilach

TIGER IN CHEVY. Frank and Bridget Egerton. Hand-carved
pine painted with gouache. 6½" high, 10½" wide.

TOYS

If the word "toy" conjures images of brightly colored plastic it's time to
look about and see what's going on. There has been a renaissance in the toy
industry. A new practicality is beginning to grasp our senses about the things
we give our children to play with. Or things we play with, ourselves. Wooden
toys are on toy shelves in profusion. They are beautiful. Simple. Healthful.
Durable. And they leave much to the child's imagination. There are stores that
sell only wooden toys—not a bit of plastic to be found.

This rebirth began with the craftsman toy maker who sold stylized buses
and cars, with gently rounded shapes and holes that simulated windows. The
natural woods were beautiful, there were no parts to break or pieces to come
apart and be swallowed. Parents, grandparents, store owners, recognized the
quality of these toys. Soon, several of the toy makers were "producing" their
objects in basements, garages, back porches and wherever they had their saws
and sanders set up.

Some toy makers have preferred to carve out their irresistible objects one by
one and they have found a ready market among the growing number of toy
collectors. All toys are not made for and used by children. There are games for
adults, paraphernalia items and replicas of antique toys. Such pieces are rapidly
becoming "art toys" and "collectors' toys." In so doing, they are encroaching
upon and wending their way into the heart of art object–sculpture. The gap
continues to close between art and craft; function and nonfunction.

LIFEGUARD. Frank and Bridget Egerton. Pine painted with gouache. 8" high, 23" wide.

EXECUTIVE TIGER. Frank and Bridget Egerton. The chair swivels. 8½" high, 6½" wide.

DECADENT CAT. Frank and Bridget Egerton. Pine painted with gouache. 7" high, 4¾" wide.

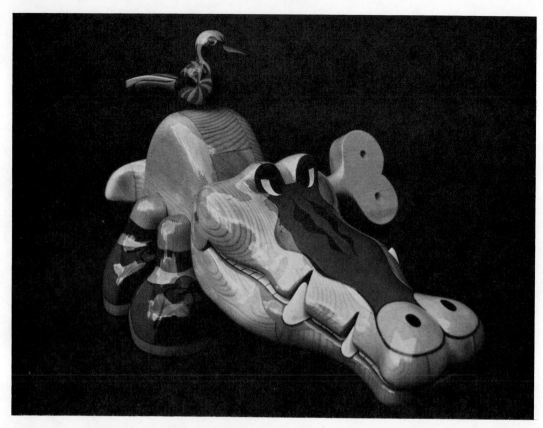

ALLIGATOR. Frank and Bridget Egerton. Pine painted with gouache. 21″ high, 22″ wide.

DECADENT CAT. Frank and Bridget Egerton. Pine painted with gouache. 6″ high, 9½″ wide. All photographs, courtesy, artists

AIRPLANE. Bill Horgos. Various hardwoods and an ivory propellor. 6" wingspread. An actual portrait of the airplane, its owner and his girl friends. Courtesy, artist

LADY ON COUCH. Bill Horgos. Boxwood. A miniature carving approximately 3" high. A tongue-in-cheek portrait of the artist's wife, Lilli. "This piece took fifty-five hours and eight surgical stitches." Courtesy, artist

39

MEN AND GIRLS. Part of a chess set. Bill Horgos. 1980. Boxwood, painted. Average size: 3" high. Courtesy, artist

PIPES 'N' BOTTLES. Bill Horgos. Mixed hardwoods. Each approximately 3" high. Paraphernalia items. Courtesy, artist

PIPES. William H. Livingston. 1979–1980. Briar. Sizes range from 5" to 7" in length.

LETTER OPENERS. William H. Livingston. Varied woods including walnut burl, eastern maple, flowering plum, zebrawood, cocobolo, osage orange, cordia and others. Photographs, artist

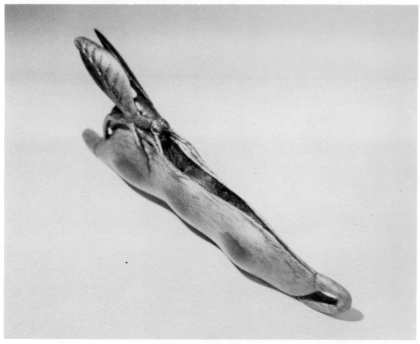

WASP ON A BEAN POD. David Carlin. 1980. Cocobolo. 4½" long. Collection, Mrs. B. Behrman, San Francisco, CA

SNAIL ON A SQUASH. David Carlin. 1980. Cocobolo. 4" long. Carlin's early pieces were often functional. These have become completely sculptural. He draws his inspiration from the Japanese net-suke. Collection, Mrs. B. Behrman, San Francisco, CA

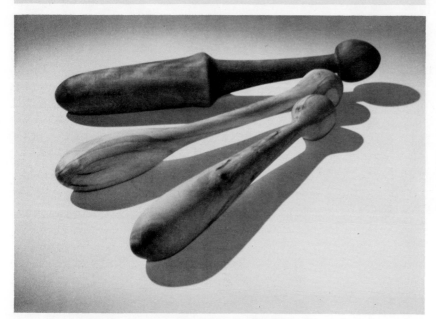

DILDOS. Ron Kent. 1978–1979. Exotic hardwoods. Overall lengths, 9" to 12". Diameter range, 1" to 2½" and 3" to 5". Courtesy, artist

EGG SCALE. Bill Chappelow. 1980. East Indian rosewood, acacia, English walnut. 5" high, 12" wide, 3½" deep. The scale is sensitive to two-hundredths of an ounce. Photograph, Dona Meilach

TALISMANS. Jack Boyd. 1979–1980. An assemblage of organic materials laminated, then carved, and engraved in the scrimshaw method. Wood, bone, horn. Secret or personal objects within the pieces pertain to the significance of the talisman's functions: hunter, fisherman, magic, and so forth. They possess magical powers. Courtesy, artist

PENCIL PODS WITH SPACE POD JARS. Steve Loar, Mahogany, birch, walnut. Also called NIGHT DEPOSITORIES. Approximately 4" high, 4" diameter. Courtesy, artist

ROCKING SERPENT. Dean Santner. 1979. Spruce and birch plywood. Koa wood rockers, maple eyes, paint. Courtesy, artist

ROCKING BIRD. Andrew J. Willner. Ash and various hardwoods 49″ high, 36″ wide. Courtesy, artist

VIKING SHIP LOG HOLDER. Neal M. Widett. Yellow pine. 35″ high, 55″ wide, 22″ deep. Photograph, Ron Harrod

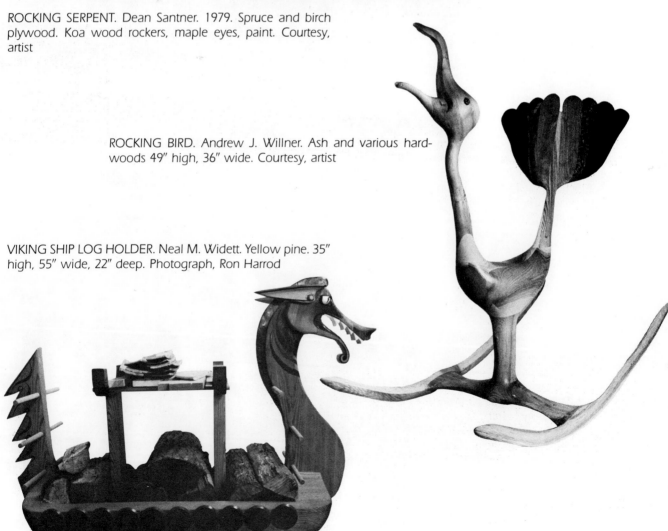

SLED I. Jim Wallace. 1976. Cherry and mild steel forged. 18"
high, 36" long, 15" wide. Collection, Mr. Ira Adler, New York

SLED V. Jim Wallace. 1980. Ash, steel, fiberglass. 17" high, 50"
long, 16" wide. Courtesy, artist

MARY'S SLED. Jim Wallace. 1980. Steam-bent walnut and
forged steel. 12" high, 40" long, 14" deep. Photograph, Doug
Long

UNICYCLE CLOWN. Jack Dohany. Hardwoods. A push toy with moving joints. Collection, Lyndon Thompson, Descanso, CA

FRENCH JUMPING JACK. Jack Dohany. Hardwoods. Painting in bright, vivid colors with a different design on each side is by Elaine Shelton and Jean Cronin. Collection, Lyndon Thompson, Descanso, CA. Photographs, Dona Meilach

FLIGHT OF FANCY AIRPLANE. Lynn Way. 1979. The plane body is poplar, the noseband and wheel rims are mahogany and walnut. The propeller, wheel hubs and struts are zebrawood. 16" long, 24" wingspan. Photograph, Nora P. Jacob

FIRE ENGINE. Hugh Gundry. 1980. 6" high, 14" long. Photograph, Dona Meilach

SKIPLOADER. Bill Chappelow. White oak, black oak and ash. 6" high, 14" long. Courtesy, artist

47

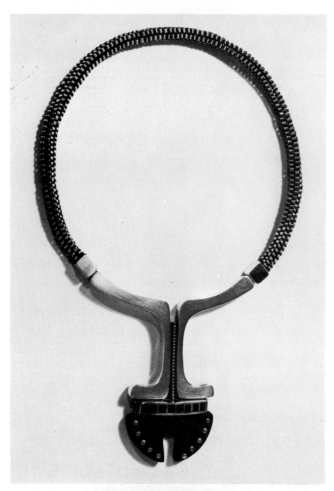

WOVEN NECKPIECE III. Pamela Allman.
1979. Padouk, sterling silver and acrylic.
Courtesy, artist

NECKLACE. Walt Zimmerman. 1978.
Mahogany and silver. Collection, Dona
Meilach

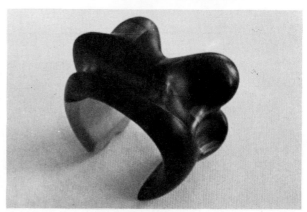

TOP: BASE PIN II. Pamela Allman. 1980.
Padouk, sterling silver. Courtesy, artist

CENTER: BRACELET. Manual A. Gomez.
Laminated colorful woods.

BELOW: NECKLACE. Kathleen Maiwald.
1979. Oak, vermilion, with jade beads.
Courtesy, artist

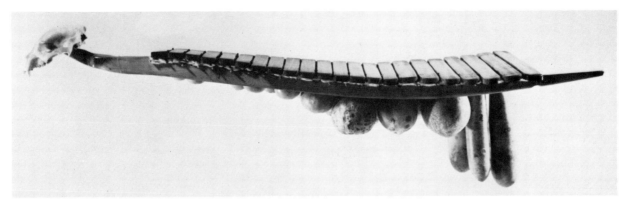

ABOVE: ZE BEAR MARIMBA. Bill and Mary Buchen. Zebrawood, birch, gourds, bear skull, felt, waxed linen. 22″ high, 70″ long, 23″ wide. Photograph, Craig E. Blair

BELOW: ROSEHORN MARIMBA. Bill and Mary Buchen. 1979. Rosewood, birch, cow horns, deerskull, felt, waxed linen. 22″ high, 14″ wide, 66″ long. Photograph, Craig E. Blair

ELK HARPS made of elkhorn, ebony, hickory, gourds, with metal strings, being played by the creators, Bill and Mary Buchen. Photograph, D. Quackenbush

49

LANDSCAPE PLATE. William Patrick. 1980. Zebra, padouk, goncalo alves, tulip. 13" diameter, ⅛" thick, laminated and turned. Courtesy, artist

MANDALA. Craig M. Kovacs. 1980. Laminated and inlaid walnut, mahogany, birch, alder, rosewood, maple and teak, lathe turned to achieve a wavy, undulating surface. 32" diameter. Courtesy, artist

WINDSURFERS. Heinz Norhausen. 1980.
Varied wood veneers used to create a
composition in wood. 3' high, 6' wide.
Collection, The Chart House, Dana Point,
CA. Courtesy, artist

DRAGON #1. Bobb Perrone. 1979. A detailed picture is developed on a birch tray by woodburning. Some portions are
stained for highlighting, then the piece is photographed and
Bobb uses the negative for making limited-edition engraved
prints. 24" square. Courtesy, artist

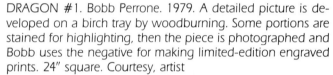

STREET IN WÜRZBURG. Jan Fleck. 1979.
Clear cedar. 24" high, 30" wide. Pyrog-
raphy and etching. Photograph, Weston
J. Ault

McCALLISTER BOX—UNTITLED. Michael N. Graham. 1980.
Imbuia, padouk, East Indian rosewood, walnut, bubinga. 10″
high, 10″ wide, 8″ deep. (For closed view, see Chapter I,
page 3.) Photograph, Robert Howell

LOADED WITH EXTRAS (detail). Michael Cooper. 1979. Laminated Australian jarrah. 41" long, 25" high, 28" wide. (See Chapter 6, page 4.)

INDIAN JAR. Giles Gilson. 1979. Inlaid and turned woods including Macassar ebony, padouk, tiger maple, birch, East Indian rosewood. 6½" high, 7½" diameter.

ROSALINE ROXBURY. Igor Givotovsky. 1972. African mahogany. 22" high, 11" wide, 2½" deep. Collection, Jim McMahon, Dorchester, MA. Photograph, artist

GALLERY DESK. Lawrence B. Hunter. 1979. Walnut. 28½" high, 6' long, 32" deep. With chair, it is 34" high and 44" deep. Collection, Art Gallery, San Diego State University, CA.

STANDING FORM #7–1–79. Doug Ayers. 1979. Honduras mahogany. 31" high, 25" wide, 3½" deep. Courtesy, artist

MR. & MRS. ERNEST CARVING AT THE OPENING. Barbara Spring. 1980. Mr. Carving: 6' high; Mrs. Carving: 5'2" high. Mr. Carving is created from cedar logs (stained); his tie is ash; Alaskan cedar is his shirt; redwood sawdust and resin make up the sweater, and the face and hands are redwood. Mrs. Carving is made from one piece of redwood; her sweater is the bark, her skirt is the sapwood and her face and hands are the interior wood. Photograph, Richard Sargent

KELP. Robert D. Mason. 1979. Spanish cedar timbers, edge-glued. 36" high, 60" wide, 4" deep. A relief panel that interprets the large algae, water and sand near the shores of San Diego. Collection, Exxon Corporation, Houston, TX. Photograph, artist

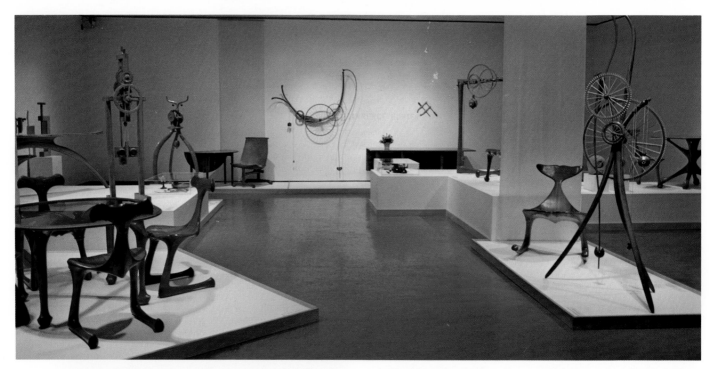

GALLERY EXHIBITION OF FURNITURE AND OBJECTS. Lawrence B. Hunter. 1980. Boehm Gallery, Palomar College, San Marcos, CA. Photograph, Dona Meilach

STANDING MIRROR AND BLANKET BOX. Sterling Johnson King. 1978–79. Oak. (See Chapter 5, page 6.)

LARGE CHAIR. J. B. Blunk. 1978 Cypress. 84" high, 40" wide, 36" deep. Courtesy, artist

DOG CAR. Frank and Bridget Egerton. 1980. Polychromed woods and natural woods. 7" high, 10½" long, 6" wide. Courtesy, artists

INVERTED BOTTLE. Stephen M. Paulsen. 1980. Cocobolo with turned and carved stopper and stand of Indian rosewood. The carved mask and draw pins are also Indian rosewood. 9" high. Courtesy, artist

Sculptor Fumio Yoshimura with his SUNFLOWERS in his New York studio. Photograph, Dona Meilach

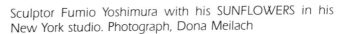

HOPPER. David L. Green. 1974. Found wood, pine and metal parts. 30" high, 14" wide, 7" deep. Photograph, artist

UNEXPLORED LANDSCAPE. Dickson Carroll. 1979. Polychromed woods carved and assembled. 16" long, 16" high, 12" deep. Courtesy, artist

SHAMAN. Michael K. Stevens. 1979. Pine and enamel. 24" high, 23" wide, 6" deep. Courtesy, artist

THE LOST HORIZON. Robert Bourdon.
1980. Honduras mahogany. 35" high,
50" wide, 4" deep. Photograph, D.
James Dee

VIKING. Heinz Norhausen. 1977. 40"
high, 30" wide. About fifteen mixed and
solid woods including Carpathian elm
burl, walnut burl, Brazilian rosewood,
holly, pernambuco, cherry, koa, zebrawood, ebony, walnut and poplar. There
is turquoise in the handle with silver
inlay. Photograph, Dona Meilach

UNTITLED. Richard Feese. 1980. Redwood and nails. 96" high, 45" wide, 48"
deep. Outdoor Sculpture, Sacramento,
CA. Courtesy, artist

SCULPTURAL TABLE. Bobby Reed Falwell. 1979. Red oak, koa, padouk, purpleheart. 16" high, 31" long, 24" deep. Courtesy, artist

ONE PIECE BOX #7. Caroline Gassner Kaplowitz. 1975. Carved from one piece of pine. 13½" high, 12" wide, 11½" deep. Collection, Dr. Martin & Mrs. Nancy Delman, Great Neck, L.I., NY

BILLOWING FORMS. Jerry Deasy. 1980. Zebrawood on a black base. Fragmented shapes. 36" wide. Courtesy, artist

DOUBLE MUSIC STAND. Andrew J. Willner. 1975. Red oak and English brown oak. 72" high. Collection, Geller Residence, Morristown, NJ

PART II
FURNITURE

3

Tables and Desks

Given the parameters of the concept "table," a flat top and supporting members, and the number of years they have been made, the style changes attest to man's inventiveness.

Today's furniture maker deals with a broad palette: sweeping clean forms and shapes, uncluttered surfaces, beautiful grains and natural finishes. There is no desire to emulate intricate carvings and rococo trims associated with historical decorative styles.

Those who lovingly laminate shapes and steam-bend flexuous forms do not pretend to compete with factory-made objects. They have, however, learned to adopt many tools of industry to make their working time more effective and to provide an extensive variety to the designs they can bring out of the wood. Die grinders, industrial planers and gluing machines and others may be used in the small studio. While these tools enable the lone furniture designer to create a finished product more efficiently, each millimeter of wood is still prepared and finished by hand processes, one process at a time. There are no production lines or schedules. Nor can large amounts of wood be purchased at quantity rates. More likely, wood sources are from felled trees found locally, however and wherever they are. The logs must be cured and prepared. Costs are time, tools, energy and tender loving care.

But the furniture maker has great freedom. He can be conservative or flamboyant. Usually he has to please only himself. When he creates for a client, the buyer usually knows the person's work and reputation and seeks him out because of it, not to bend the artist's creativity to his will. If the artist feels stifled by someone else's design imposition, he may reject the commission. Even when furniture makers design for church or corporate commissions, they aim to please themselves as well as their clients.

The handmade table or other furniture object is an original work of art. No two can be exactly the same. It is a functional sculpture and the use and daily enjoyment of it are almost incidental bonuses.

The experienced furniture maker is, without doubt, a virtuoso in wood. Each component part must be perfectly shaped and planned. No "accidents" can happen in design without a reaction. With a nonfunctional piece, of

TABLE AND CHAIRS. Lawrence B. Hunter. 1979. Cherry with glass top and a hand-carved rim. Beluga whale chairs. Stack laminations. Photograph, artist

course, the sculptor can take advantage of an accidentally miscut element and work it into a final theme or shape.

Designers whose work is illustrated have experienced their accidents and their failures. They have learned their woodworking lessons well, either formally or informally.

It is pleasing to report that many furniture makers who, only a few years ago, were creating one or two pieces a year, as time permitted from other jobs, are discovering a market and channels for sales that exist through galleries, decorators and architects. It is now possible to combine avocation and vocation. Union Woodworks in Vermont and Satisfaction-Promise Woodworking Company in California each grew in similar ways—through a variety of con-

COFFEE TABLE. Bill Keyser. 1978. Elm-log slab top with constructed and laminated base using serpentine cherry, maple and walnut stripes. The base is molded plywood with veneered maple on top and bottom. The cantilevered top is supported at one end by the connecting wooden discs. Photograph, Robert Kushner

tacts one commission led to another; reputations were established for customized and limited-edition pieces; each expanded, rented larger space, hired helpers and perhaps formed partnerships. Yet, to keep a working shop going year around, they try to have a line of production pieces on the front saw. Satisfaction-Promise produces cabinets for stereo and other electronic equipment; Union Woodworks builds a line of architectural furniture.

The approach to design differs among those interviewed. Some people adhere to one design concept and push it as far as they can. They constantly revise and refine until they are ready to move to a new concept. Others explore the nature of one material. Alan Friedman, for example, has created tables and lamps from Finnish plywood, a material not usually associated with fine furniture.

Sterling Johnson King's cocktail tables take their inspiration from the mountains and his love of surfing. Andrew Willner's ideas are born in nature, too: mountains and water, plus fantasies from dreams and nursery rhymes. Cloud shapes are incorporated into the desks made by Robert and Joanne Herzog. Real objects are interpreted as furniture in a tongue-in-cheek approach by John W. McNaughton.

The log frequently suggests the form for artists Jon Brooks and Howard Werner. If it were possible to give each man the identical log with identical properties, each would undoubtedly design a completely different piece. Such is the essence of the creative mind and hand.

DINING TABLE. Howard Werner. Walnut. 29″ high, 6½′ long,
3½′ wide.

COFFEE TABLE. Howard Werner. Walnut. 17″ high, 4′ long,
2½′ wide. Courtesy, artist

WAVE TABLE #7. Two views. Peter Michael Adams. 1979. Walnut. 18" high, 72" long, 32" wide. Photograph, Dan Bailey

The series of Wave Tables was developed from exploratory design lines drawn over and under and between the end view perspective of a group of oil storage tanks. From this search for form the function of the table was incorporated, so that function followed form as opposed to the Bauhaus credo that form follows function. Photograph, Dan Bailey

BIG THURSDAY. Sterling King. 1980. Maple and walnut. The top was stained blue and airbrushed for a water pattern, then finished with lacquer. 15" high, 5½' long, 2½' wide. The inspiration is from the artist's love of the sea and the relationship between the ocean and the shore. Photographs, Dona Meilach

COFFEE TABLE. Kevin M. Irvin. 1980. Willow and soft maple. Bent lamination. 16" high, 53" long, 17" wide. Courtesy, artist

DINING TABLE. Michael Goldfinger and John Wall. Union Woodworks. 1979. Black walnut, bird's-eye maple, glass. 29" high, 80" long, 40" wide. Collection, Anne Foss and Peter Feig, Avon, CT

CLOUD TABLE. JAWAR (James Rannefeld). Media Seven Design Group. 1980. Laminated and sculptured oak. 17" high, 48" long, 15" wide. Courtesy, artist

PENLAND TABLE. Jon Brooks, Walnut, pine and ebony. 18″ high, 50″ long, 18″ wide. Photograph, Woody Packard

WESTERN SHIRT TABLE. Bruce Decker. 1980. The body is ash; the shirt yoke, collar and stripes are East Indian rosewood; the arrow points are purpleheart. 20″ high, 32″ long, 22″ wide. Courtesy, artist

SIDE TABLE. Chuck Masters. Cherry and walnut with supports of bent and laminated mahogany. 30" high, 53" long, 29" wide. The "imposed warp" is carved to achieve the lift at the split. Courtesy, artist

STAR TABLE. Bob Trotman. Walnut, curly maple, ash, mahogany. 25" high, 16" long, 12" wide. When the drawer is opened, acrylic resin stars line the drawer bottom. The "stars" are carved from the wood, then filled in with resin and sanded back for the inlay effect. Photograph, Timothy D. Smith

OPPOSITE, TOP: SIDEBOARD. Ed Dadey. Padouk. 36" high, 54" long, 18" wide. Courtesy, artist

OPPOSITE, BELOW: TABLE. Ed Dadey. Maple. 35" high, 66" long, 33" wide. Courtesy, artist

DINING TABLE FOR EIGHT. With triple seat benches. Jack Rogers Hopkins. 1979. Oak, cherry, shedua, walnut, Honduras mahogany. Table: 30" high, 6'6" long, 34" wide. Collection, Mr. and Mrs. Arthur Taub, Encino, CA

A custom three-part table designed for storability. The three-section top comes off and stores in a standard that holds them and also screens the collapsible base (BELOW). The entire top and base store beneath a 16-inch wide counter which holds various cabinets. One section of the table top becomes a front cabinet panel. Courtesy, artist

DINING SET. David G. Flatt. 1980. Walnut. Table: 31" high, 72" long, 42" wide. Chair: seat, 19" high, 17½" wide; back height, 31½". Courtesy, artist

WRAPAROUND WRITING DESK. Jack Rogers Hopkins. Shedua. 29" high, 6' long, 7' wide. The desk is made in three units, which can be separated. The top and leg sections are also made to be separated. When the sections are assembled, the writer for whom the desk was commissioned can work in a **U**-shape with his work on three sides. Collection, Mr. Leo Meyer, Hayward, CA

CONFERENCE TABLE. Saumitra Lewis Buchner. 1980. Ash. 16' long. The wood understructure for the ½-inch-thick plate-glass top is designed and built on the same principles as a boat hull. Photograph, Schopplein Studios

Notes Mr. Buchner: "I feel that the corporations of today are beginning to support the crafts in much the same way that the religious institutions have in the past and will continue to do so." His company, Satisfaction-Promise Woodworking Co., delivers what its name implies, and they "have the opportunity to work on projects using a wide variety of premium materials and for which we are paid well enough to take the time necessary to work to our capacity."

THE LIBERTY DINING TABLE AND CHAIRS. John Makepeace. 1978. Photographed in the Great Hall at Parnham House, Beaminster, Dorset, England. Collection, Liberty & Co.

LOW TABLE FOR THE RED LIBRARY, LONGLEAT HOUSE. John Makepeace. 1979–1980. Commissioned by the Sixth Marquess of Bath, England. Photographs, P. E. and M. E. Payne

GAME TABLE. Robert E. March. 1979–1980. Walnut burl top. 29" high, 42" square.

SIDE TABLE. Robert E. March. 1979. Cherry. 29" high, 60" long, 18" wide. Photographs, John I. Russell

PARNHAM EDITION TABLES. The John Makepeace Furniture Workshops at Parnham House, Beaminster, Dorset, England. Each table is signed by the individual craftsman. Photograph, Jeremy Whitaker

Custom-designed and limited-edition tables or designs that are easily altered slightly for an individual customer have become readily marketable objects for many woodwork studios.

C-LEG TABLE. Michael Goldfinger and John Wall. Union Woodworks, Vermont. Strip laminated constructed of Honduras mahogany and black walnut. 29" high, 46" diameter. Courtesy. Union Woodworks

TABLE. Alan Friedman. 1980. Padouk with Danish fir plywood top. 30" high, 43½" diameter.

Friedman prefers a plywood with a spruce and fir mix from Finland. The color ranges are from pale blond to a rich red chestnut, all with swirling, intricate grain patterns. "It's a challenging and interesting material to investigate for furniture design." Collection, David S. Hamburger, Los Angeles, CA; Photographs, Bob Lantz
RIGHT: Side view.

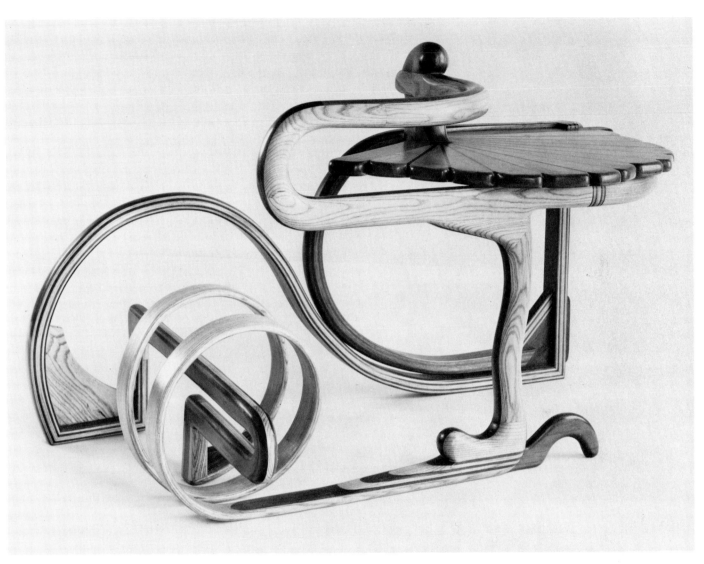

TABLE. Gary Galbraith. 1978. Walnut, oak, ash, maple. 38"
high, 40" wide, 34" deep.

Galbraith writes: "The diverse range of forming processes
that are the heritage of wood offers exciting engineering
problems encompassing the ability to design a structure in
space and to visually express an idea as form. I create pieces
that suggest the activation of interior space." Courtesy, artist

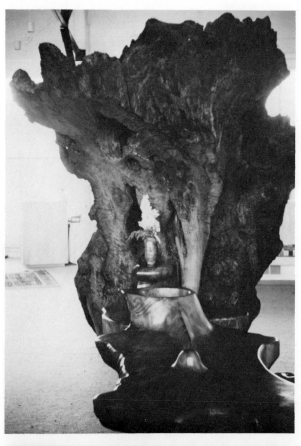

OPPOSITE, TOP: TABLE. Garry K. Bennett. Wood, metal, glass. 30" high, 54" diameter.

OPPOSITE, BELOW: BUFFET. Garry K. Bennett. Mixed woods polychromed and natural. Glass top. 30" high, 60" long, 27" wide. Courtesy, artist

9-PIECE TABLE ENCLOSURE. J. B. Blunk. 1979. Redwood. The enclosure forms an 18'-by-24' oval ring. Twenty-five people can sit on stools around and within for informal eating. The high sculptural form (LEFT) is at the end of the table ring; the entire piece is like a sculptural environment that dominates Green's Restaurant interior at Fort Mason, San Francisco. Courtesy, artist

ROPE COCKTAIL TABLE (detail).

John McNaughton brings to furniture design a background as a woodworker, sculptor, industrial designer and teacher. "My work has to go beyond being well crafted and a nice table. It has to be an art object which makes a statement, a message with impact." He is strongly influenced by Claes Oldenburg's radical modification of the scale of a recognizable object, and "humor and whimsy play an important part in my work."

McNaughton may work from a series of sketches, and/or use full-size sketches, and models. Often, he will use foam rubber to mold a prototype and to think through unforeseen problems as they arise.

74

ROPE COCKTAIL TABLE. John W. McNaughton. 1979. Mahogany, laminated plywood. 18" high, 53" long, 18" deep. Collection, Ball State University Art Department, Muncie, IN

RIPSAW TABLE. John W. McNaughton. 1978. Laminated plywood, partridge-wood. 16" high, 48" long, 15" wide. Private collection

THE KNIFE TABLE. John W. McNaughton. 1979. Cocktail size with blades that extend for extra serving area. 14" high, 52" long, 14" deep. Collection, Mr. and Mrs. Gene Warren, Evansville, IN. Courtesy, artist

75

RAM TABLE. Andrew J. Willner. Mahogany, walnut and glass. 36" diameter.

ARCHIPELAGO COFFEE TABLE. Andrew J. Willner. Cherry and glass. 16" high, 36" square.

NURSERY RHYMES TABLE. Andrew J. Willner. Cherry and found object. 28" high, 24" diameter.

VOLCANO TABLE. Andrew J. Willner. Mahogany and maple. 30" high, 22" diameter.

CONFECTION END TABLE. Andrew J. Willner. Red oak. 30" high. Collection, Schwartz Residence, Englewood, NJ. All photographs courtesy, artist

WALNUT WHIRL COCKTAIL TABLE.
Margery Eleme Goldberg. 1979. Walnut,
oak, cherry and mahogany. 18" high, 24"
square. Courtesy, artist

COFFEE TABLE. Stephen L. Casey. 1980.
Mahogany with lacquer finish. "The
same crispness and sculptural quality
could be made in plastic, metal or glass.
It's the form that is important." Courtesy,
artist

COFFEE TABLE. David Holzapfel. Ash
with acrylic base. 17" high, 5' long, 30"
wide. Courtesy, artist

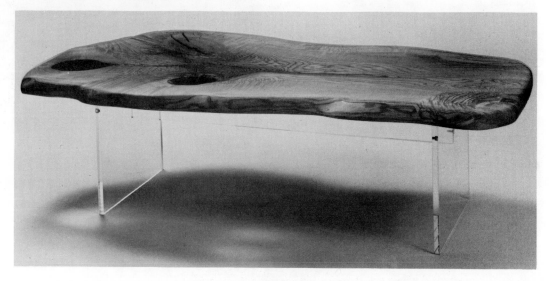

QUARTER ROUND COFFEE TABLE.
David G. Flatt. 1980. Red oak. 15" high,
4' long, 3' wide. Courtesy, artist

RETURN OF THE 5,000-LB. MAN. Phillip
Bailey. 1976. Mahogany. 29" high. Courtesy, artist

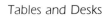

TABLE. Carl E. Johnson. 1979. White oak.
18" high, 22" square. Courtesy, artist

79

SIDE TABLE. Mark S. Levin. Walnut. 24" high, 20" diameter. Courtesy, artist

COFFEE TABLE. Mark S. Levin. White oak. 16" high, 38" long, 38" wide. Courtesy, artist

"TWO" TABLE. JAWAR (James Rannefeld). Media Seven Design Group. Laminated oak interior or hole is polychromed. 24" high, 20" square. Courtesy, artist

BUTCHER BLOCK TABLE. George A. Sabosik. 1980. Sugar maple. 32" high, 22" long. 19" wide. Courtesy, artist

80

COCKTAIL TABLE. Anton Marc. 1979. Steam-bent and laminated-oak construction. 16" high, 54" long, 14" wide. Courtesy, artist

COFFEE TABLE. Ejner C. Pagh. Walnut. 18" high, 64" long, 26" wide. Courtesy, Mindscape Gallery, Evanston, IL. Photograph, artist

TOP: FRIENDSHIP TABLE. William M. Richardson. Mahogany. 29" high, 40" square. Chairs in mahogany and leather. Custom-designed pieces are made so tops and materials can be changed. Courtesy, artist

TABLE AND CHAIRS. Joseph A. Agate and Fred Wildnauer. 1980. Mahogany and glass. Handwoven fabric upholstery by Patti Mitchem. The designers work closely with the architects. Courtesy, Agate/Wildnauer Associates

QUEEN ANNE TABLE. Design by Susan Chandler Wilson. Execution in wood by Neal M. Widett. The table is mahogany. The queen (see detail) is carved and peened in pine, with some painting and gold leafing added. 30" high, 84" long, 40" wide. Photograph, Ron Harrod

83

GALLERY DESK. Lawrence B. Hunter. 1980. Walnut. Tapered lamination. 32" high, 72" long, 36" wide. The seat swivels 360°. Collection, San Diego State University, San Diego, CA. Photograph, artist

DESK. Garry K. Bennett. 1980. Wood and aluminum. 29"
high, 61" long, 30"' wide. Courtesy, artist

DESK. Garry K. Bennett. 1980. Mixed woods and fabricated
aluminum. 30" high, 60" long, 24" wide. Courtesy, artist

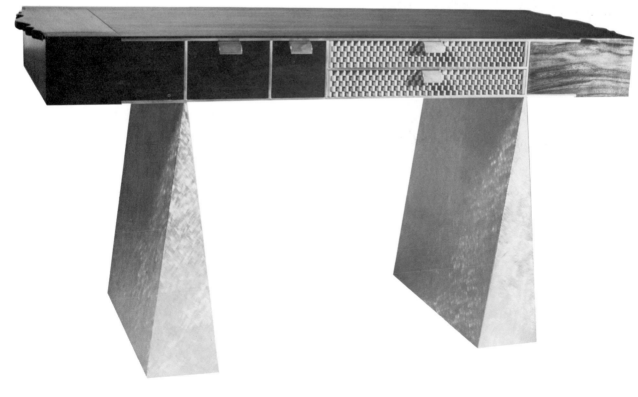

RECEPTION DESK. Jack Rogers Hopkins. Walnut, oak, cherry, maple. 36" high, 6' long, 5' deep. Collection, San Diego State University, Art Department, San Diego, CA

DESK AND CHAIR—CONTINUUM SERIES. Robert C. Whitley. Walnut and bird's-eye maple. Desk: 29" high, 64" long, 30" wide. Chair: 37" high, 24½" wide, 25½" deep. Courtesy, artist

DESK. Robert E. March. 1980. Two views. Hickory. 29″ high, 62″ long, 26″ deep. Courtesy, artist

EL MORRO DESK WITH MATADOR II CHAIR. Michael Coffey. Mozambique wood. Desk: 37″ high, 68″ wide, 18″ deep. Chair: 25″ high, 24″ wide, 23″ deep. Courtesy, artist

Erik Gronborg uses avocado wood native to his area in southern California as opposed to usual furniture woods. His desk, drawing tables (see page 127), chests and chairs utilize the inherent form found in a log. "If a piece of wood has a bend in it, use it," he maintains. The furniture has a presence, a personality, a humor that you notice as you study it. He emphasizes structure and the joints; he does not hide them. Many joints also function so the piece may be easily dismantled and the parts played with, as an oversized Playskool® toy. Each curve, each corner and joint have a tactile quality and shaping: the hand-carved hinges and surprise opening and closing devices suggest a Rube Goldberg approach. The fantasy form pieces invite you to touch them, play with them, rub them and not take them seriously. But they are so functional, and at the same time sculptural, that they wield a powerful impact and illustrate the artist's control of his ideas and medium.

WRITING DESK. Closed and open views. Erik Gronborg. 1979–1980. Avocado wood. As the writing surface is dropped, the hand-carved hinge slides forward and becomes a supportive member. 42" high, 24" wide, 26" deep.

HALL DESK. Erik Gronborg. 1979–1980.
Avocado wood. 68" high, 22" wide, 16"
deep.

DESK WITH BENCH. Erik Gronborg. 1979–1980. Avocado
wood. Observe the hand-carved holding latch at the top, a
dedication to emphasize the desk devices rather than hide
them as hardware. 54" high, 32" wide, 27" deep. Photographs, Erik Gronborg

DESK AND CHAIR. Charles B. Cobb. 1979. Hawaiian koa and African zebrawood with ebony dowels. 48" high, 6' long, 34" wide. The chair is Koa with ebony pegs. The suede-upholstered seat matches the suede-lined drawers. Photograph, Bill Galloway

STUDENT DESK AND CHAIR. Jack Rogers Hopkins. 1980. The major wood is cherry. The desk top and chair back are laminates of walnut, rosewood, Honduras mahogany, oak, shedua and maple. The top flips up for storage within. Desk: 30" high, 24" wide, 19" deep. Chair: 27" high, 19" wide, 17" deep. Photograph, Dona Meilach

ROLLTOP DESK. Sara Jaffe. 1979. Koa and New Guinea mahogany. 29" high in front, 38" high at back. 36" long, 27" deep. Photograph, Craig Buchanan

AVANTI II. JAWAR (James Rannefeld). Media Seven Design Group. 1980. Tambour desk in koa and ash. 37" high, 48" wide, 32" deep. Courtesy, artist

JOE'S DESK. Michael Goldfinger and John Wall. Union Woodworks. Honduras mahogany, African mahogany. Tambour construction, frame and panel side. 50" high, 50" wide, 36" deep. Photograph, Robert Barrett

CLOUD DESK. Robert and Joanne Herzog. 1979. New Guinea narra and bird's-eye maple. 48" wide. Photograph, Bill Galloway

4

Chairs and Other Seating

C hairs. They are temporary containers for people. How do they hold us? How do they shape us? How do we shape them?

 We have come a long way since chairs were only a place to rest and design was a Spartan expression of function. Seating as sculpture is a guiding principle for today's contemporary chair designers.

 Next to stretched-out or curled-up in a prone sleeping position, sitting is the position in which most of us spend a majority of our waking hours. Sitting positions change, depending upon our activities. We sit in a straight-back chair at the breakfast table or at a desk. We lean forward from a stool at a counter. We may slump in a soft chair when we lounge. We sit differently when we're behind the wheel of a car. Think about various sitting positions during the day and you can not only appreciate the lack of constancy in the chairs we use, but also marvel at their constancy.

 The furniture designer must consider the myriad aspects of sitting before he even commits pencil to paper to sketch his vision. He must understand the chair's function, the shape of the spine in relation to the chair ("ergonomics," the study of the problems of people in adjusting to their environment), body scale, space and materials. With so many aspects to consider, it is little wonder so few chairs satisfy every person. Additionally, an individual judges a chair's comfort based on his height, and the length of his legs.

 The forty-five examples shown were selected from a marvelous variety submitted of approximately three hundred photographs of seating forms. Judging consisted of predetermined factors: craftsmanship, practicality, plus "The New Wave" premise established for this book.

 Among the examples that appear to meet the standards of high craftsmanship, including joinery, bends, laminations and finishes, are some that have extreme technical achievements. The designers have gone beyond the often preconceived notions of normal assembly, laminates and bends. Some chairs appear to be cantilevered and suspended in space.

BENCH. Garry K. Bennett. Dyed redwood. 21" high, 69" long, 14½" wide. Courtesy, artist

APHRODITE. Michael Coffey. Rocking lounge chair of Mozambique wood, 54" high, 90" long, 28" deep. Courtesy, artist

It was impossible to actually sit in all the chairs, so the question of comfort is rhetorical. Nor are all designs outrageous. Many are only slight departures from tradition and in their way may be considered conservative, compared to others.

It was essential, imperative, to keep design tastes in perspective and not to select for the sake of novelty. Traditional styles were rejected only because they did not represent the idea of chair design along new lines. I hope that each example will sustain itself as practical and that all together they will illustrate the broad spectrum in which today's contemporary chair designer develops and departs for and from his conceptualization of "chair."

WESTERN ROCKER. Sterling King. 1978. Walnut with top-grain cowhide. 40" high, 42" long, 28" wide. Courtesy, artist

ABOVE LEFT: ATOMIC ARM CHAIR. Bob Trotman. Honduras mahogany, walnut, dogwood. 29" high.

ABOVE, RIGHT: NEW WAVE SIDE CHAIR. Bob Trotman. Honduras mahogany, walnut, maple. 38" high.

RIGHT: ATOMIC STOOL. Bob Trotman. Mahogany, walnut, maple, resin inlaid stars. Traditional joinery emphasizes the way the pieces of wood penetrate each other. 24" high. All photographs, Paul Lemmons

"I am very interested in a symbolic, subliminal image of human consciousness when I design furniture," says Bob Trotman. "Furniture physically complements our bodies. Chairs and stools support us, tables hold things up and serve us, or provide a common ground for the people seated around them. Even the wood, in its accumulated growth, seems an image of human consciousness."

ROCKING CHAIR. Jack Rogers Hopkins. Shedua. 36" high, 24" wide, 30" deep. Collection, Mrs. John V. Wise, Peak Island, ME. Photographs, artist

MRS. HOPKINS'S CAPTAIN'S CHAIR. Jack Rogers Hopkins. Koa wood and fabric. The wraparound back was inspired by a captain's chair. The tripod back leg with two small legs evolved in an effort to depart from the usual four-leg design. 29" high, 26" wide, 25" deep. Collection, Mrs. Jack Rogers Hopkins, Spring Valley, CA

COUCH. Robert E. March. 1980. Padouk. Hand-woven fabric by Heather Merrick. 36" high, 96" long, 36" wide. Photograph, John I. Russell

ABOVE, LEFT: WINDSOR CLOUD CHAIR (CUMULUS). Mark Lindquist. 1979. Cherry burl, spalted maple, bird's-eye maple, ebony, padouk. 38" high, 27" wide, 16½" deep. From "New Hand-made Furniture" exhibit, American Craft Museum. Courtesy, artist

ABOVE, RIGHT: TONGUE CHAIR. Alan Siegel. 1979. Paint on white maple. 31½" high, 21" wide, 28" deep. Courtesy, Nancy Hoffman Gallery, New York

RIGHT MATADOR I. Michael Coffey. Mozambique wood. 30" high, 22" wide, 24" deep. Courtesy, artist

THRONE CHAIR—SERIES II. Three views. Robert C. Whitley. LEFT: side view; LEFT BELOW: front view. Curly maple with bird's-eye maple and figured walnut back splats and ebony pegs. Joints are designed so there is no dependency upon glue, and there is an allowance for expansion and contraction of the woods.

RIGHT BELOW: Upside-down view showing the bottom detailing of the Throne Chair. Courtesy, artist

CONTOUR CHAIR. Hugh Wesler. 1979. Walnut with leather upholstery. Coopered construction with layered and carved groove details. 24" high, 26" wide, 26" deep. Courtesy, artist

BELOW: SPLIT TUBE CHAIR. Two views. Hugh Wesler. Bird's-eye maple. The tubes are lathe turned, then split. Coopered and assembled over a frame. 24" high, 24" wide, 24" deep. Courtesy, artist

TÊTE-À-TÊTE. Jon Brooks. Walnut. 32"
high, 72" long, 48" wide. Photograph,
Woody Packard

MANTA RAY CHAIR. Jon Brooks. Walnut.
29" high, 42" wide, 47" deep. Photograph, Woody Packard

LOVE SEAT. Howard Werner. Poplar burl.
42" high, 66" wide, 42" deep. Courtesy,
artist

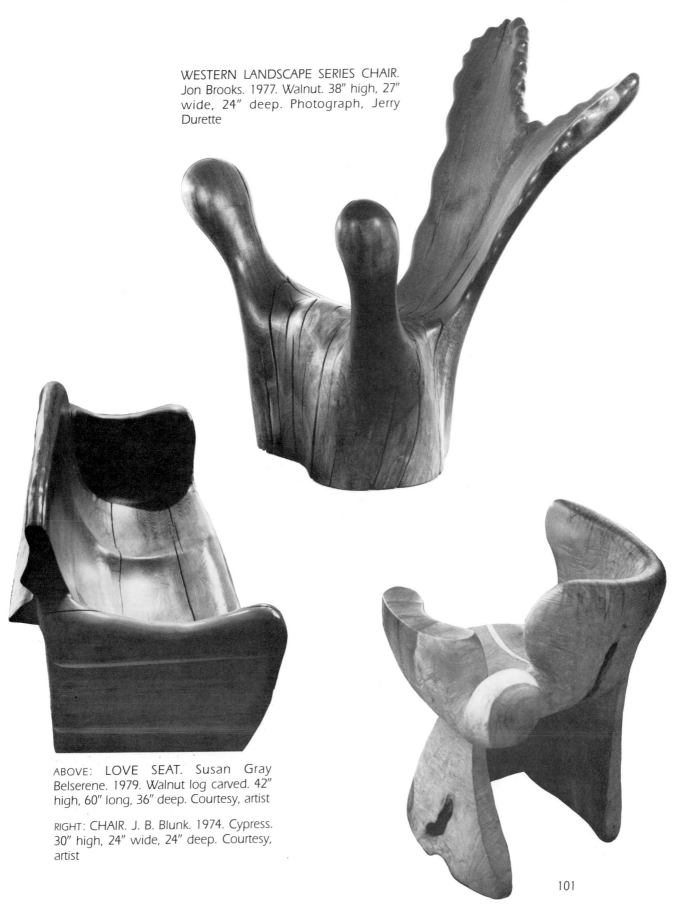

WESTERN LANDSCAPE SERIES CHAIR. Jon Brooks. 1977. Walnut. 38" high, 27" wide, 24" deep. Photograph, Jerry Durette

ABOVE: LOVE SEAT. Susan Gray Belserene. 1979. Walnut log carved. 42" high, 60" long, 36" deep. Courtesy, artist

RIGHT: CHAIR. J. B. Blunk. 1974. Cypress. 30" high, 24" wide, 24" deep. Courtesy, artist

FLOATING BACK DINING CHAIR. Rick Pohlers. Walnut with square ebony pegs. Handwoven Italian cord seat. 42″ high, 18″ wide, 19″ deep. Courtesy, artist

BELOW, LEFT: OAK CHAIR. Robert E. March, 48″ high, 24″ wide, 30″ deep.

BELOW, RIGHT: PADOUK CHAIR. Robert E. March. 48″ high, 24″ wide, 30″ deep. Photographs, John I. Russell

"ROCKET SLED" SPRING ROCKER. Bruce LePage. 1980. Laminated hard maple and forged steel. 48" high. Courtesy, artist

BELOW, LEFT: ROCKER. William Tickel. 1978. Walnut and koa. Inlay of zebrawood over rosewood. 52" high, 26" wide, 36" deep. Photograph, Mark Archer

BELOW, RIGHT: ARM CHAIR. William Tickel. 1979. Walnut and oak. Inlay of zebrawood over bubinga. 54" high, 25" wide, 32" deep. Photograph, Mark Archer

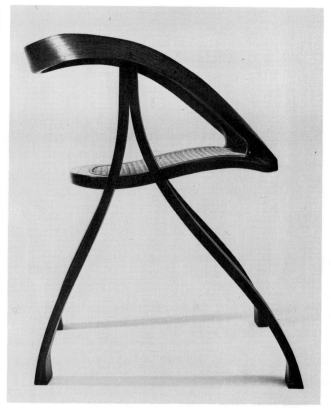

RIBBON-BACK CHAIR. John Wall and Michael Goldfinger. Union Woodworks. 1980. Honduras mahogany. One of a set of eight chairs and three stools. Collection, Mr. and Mrs. W. E. McClatatch

BENTWOOD CLIENT CHAIR. Robson Lindsay Splane, Jr. 1979. Teak. Photograph, Michael Cameti

ARM CHAIR. David G. Flatt. Walnut. 31" high. Courtesy, artist

CANTILEVER CHAIR. David G. Flatt. Walnut. 31½" high. Courtesy, artist

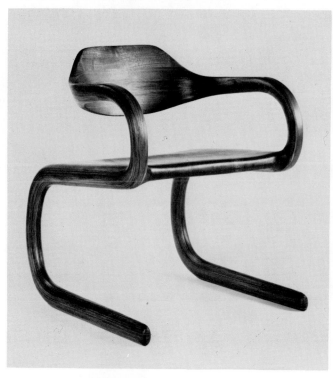

CHESS SET. John Makepeace Designs and Workshop. 1978.
Ebony and holly table with an ebony chair. Courtesy, artist

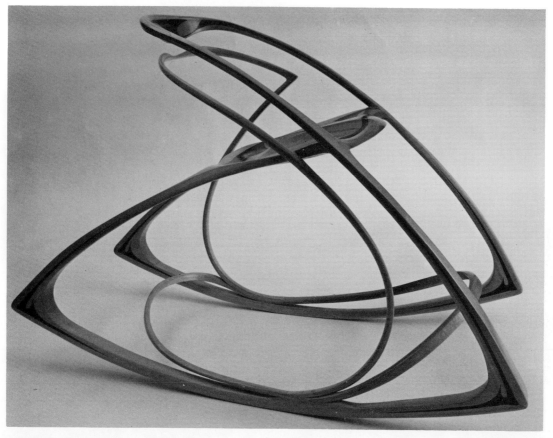

DELIGHT. Martha Rising. 1979. Maple, padouk, purpleheart.
34" high, 23½" wide, 54" deep.

TEMPEST. Two views. Martha Rising.
1979. Shedua, curly ash, brown oak,
rosewood. Photographs, Dona Meilach

RIGHT: KANGAROO ROCKER #1. Terry Schwab. 1979. Cherry. 35½" high, 19" wide, 25" deep. Courtesy, artist

BELOW: ROCKER. Ken Dieringer. 1979. Walnut. Photograph, Peter C. Tag

ABOVE: SLAT-BACK BENCH. Steve Voorheis. 1975. Maple and pine. A contemporary adaptation of a Shaker design. 34" high, 46" long, 19" wide. Courtesy, artist

RIGHT: CHAIR. Robert W. Scott. 1980. Cherry. 24" high. Compound laminate bends. Veneer bending sliced. Photograph, Vicki Scuri

ROCKING CHAIR. Giles Gilson. Padouk. The chair may be dismantled into its five basic parts (shown below without the seat) plus the dowels and bolts. 24" high, 35" wide, 39" deep. Photograph, Rich Siciliano

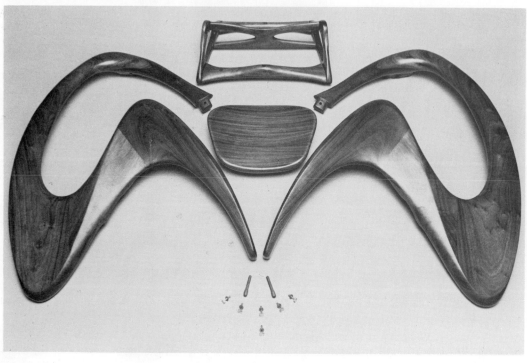

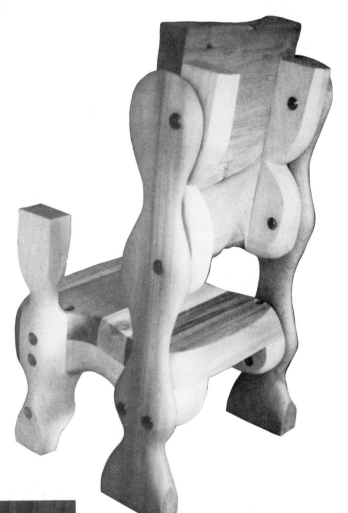

BOLTED CHAIR #1. Leonard C. Cave. 1979. Mahogany and bolts. 42" high, 28" wide, 24" deep.

BOLTED CHAIR #2. Leonard C. Cave. 1980. Mahogany, maple, satinwood, birch, and bolts. Photographs, artist

Leonard Cave assembles the chair parts in his basement workshop, where he is surrounded by his wood and stone sculptures. Photograph, Dona Meilach

"These chairs are conceived to be functional as well as contemplative forms. They establish a contact I want to make with the viewer. From this sense of understanding, the formal aspect becomes most important. The use of men and space as a compositional balance and the relationships of the forms to the requirements of function are exciting aspects to me. To fulfill the functional requirements and not compromise the aesthetics demands is important."

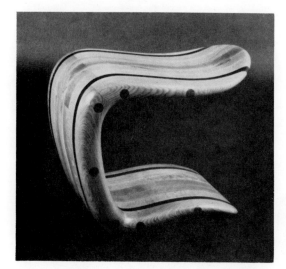

BENCH. Mark S. Levin. White oak and
padouk. 18″ high, 23″ wide, 12″ deep.
Courtesy, artist

SAFETY PIN CHAIR. Jeffrey T. McCaffrey.
Cherry with fabric sling. 5′ high, 6′ long,
3′ deep. Courtesy, artist

STOOL. Karen Hazama. 1979. Padouk
and walnut. 30″ high, 16″ wide, 12″
deep. Courtesy, artist

EXECUTIVE CHAIR. Bill Keyser. 1975. Walnut. Photograph, Robert Kushner

ROCKER. Frank E. Cummings. Japanese oak with lignum vitae bearings and ivory detailings. African goatskin covering. 42" high, 40" wide, 24" deep. Photograph, Kenneth Naversen

FOLDING CHAIRS. Saumitra Lewis Buchner. Red Elm. Walnut-topped table with elm edging and cottonwood base. Table by Dick Sellew. Courtesy, Satisfaction-Promise Woodworking Co.

5
Cabinets and Other Furnishings

The need for specific furniture pieces is timeless: tables, chairs, desks, cabinets. Their styles may change, the materials vary, the scales differ, but their need is constant.

Other furnishings do change. Some are fads or may be used by only a segment of a society. A new object is born as the need arises. Since I researched my earlier book, "Creating Modern Furniture," there have been subtle changes in the objects made. The declining popularity of the music stand was most obvious. During the 1970–75 period, the music stand was pervasive. It was a beginning assignment in furniture-design classes because it could encompass various joinery techniques as well as laminating, bending, carving and so forth. It did not have to satisfy sitting, eating heights or comfort needs. It lent itself to a free, imaginative use of the materials in a sculptural manner. The ideas could be as bizarre or reserved as the maker desired. Almost any variation of the form could hold music.

Perhaps the music-stand makers are playing with other instruments because, this time, cradles were submitted in abundance. There were plant stands, too, but few were unusual or different from one another.

Cabinetry, however, was exciting whether made to be free standing, placed against a wall or designed as part of a total environment. There was a marked departure from the rigid rectangular or square cabinet with the straight slab construction. And, unlike the table, the cabinet surface was often softened and relieved by a decorative treatment such as veneer inlays or carved, undulating shaping accomplished by laminating up, then subtracting portions. Handles, pulls and hinged joinery were integrated with the design rather than added on with alien materials. The wood was explored to a fuller potential and beauty.

Design details in cabinetry derived from traditional sources were used freely, but with tasteful restraint. The open-side construction in the chest by Michael Pearce has a source in Japanese cabinetry. The ultimate inspiration from the Japanese is the KIMONO CABINET (opposite), itself a kimono, by Hugh Wesler.

Doors were acknowledged to pose a problem. Craftsmen who fashioned them completely of exotic woods discovered that the wood checked and glued edges separated when doors were installed and subjected to unpredictable

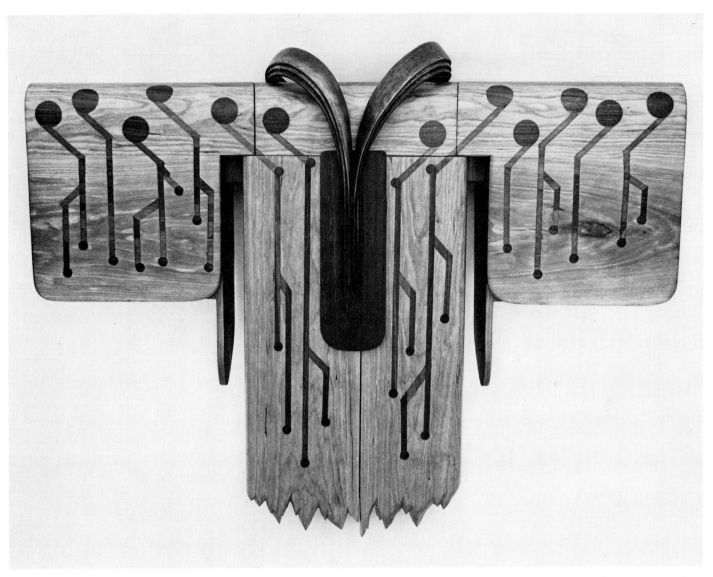

KIMONO CABINET. Hugh Wesler. 1979. Cherry with walnut inlay. Ammonia-bent walnut collar. 24" high, 26" wide, 8" deep. The cabinet is wall hung; the tops of the sleeves open upward, the sleeve bottoms open downward to reveal two compartments in each sleeve. The kimono body has doors that swing outward to 90°. Courtesy, artist

STORAGE UNIT. Two views, closed and open. John Makepeace Design and Workshop, 1978. Plied birch. Twelve trefoil-shaped drawers of three different depths are cantilevered and pivoted from a stainless steel post fixed at ground level into a spreading foot. Each drawer has a pastel-colored acrylic base. Courtesy, artist

changes of weather and climate. A door made in a coastal area workshop, then installed in a desert home, resulted in too many headaches, remakes and repairs. The majority of doors submitted were not so inspirational except for those where leaded glass was incorporated (see page 252)—and that is a subject in itself.

Lawrence B. Hunter, known for free-standing sculptural clocks, evolved new design concepts for wall-hung clocks that are spectacular. Frank E. Cummings carries the hand-carved clock into another realm with ivory gears so

CHEST OF DRAWERS. Two views, closed and open. Michael Pearce. Koa and shedua. 54″ high, 34″ wide, 18″ deep. Skeletal frame and exposed drawer construction. Courtesy, artist

decorative that each is like a miniature sculpture that could be successful all by itself.

I have included the more traditional example of the airplane interior by Paul Runge to emphasize that such commissions are now available to the custom-furniture designer as part of the new wave for artistic woodworkers to ride in the 1980s. There are corporate commissions as lucrative and important as the patronage of the arts by the church. You will observe innovation in styles in this context, too.

CORNER-HUNG CABINET. Michael Coffey. Butternut. 80" high, 47" wide, 29" deep. Designed to hold all stereo components except the speakers, plus 150 records. Courtesy, artist

BOARD-ROOM SHELF. Bill Keyser. 1978. Cherry, mahogany, maple, padouk, ramin and rosewood. 8' high, 11' wide. The triangular-shaped sections are of a hollow-rib construction and a particle board skin. The surface is veneered with thin tapered strips of the various species. The three sections are bolted together. Photograph, Robert Kushner

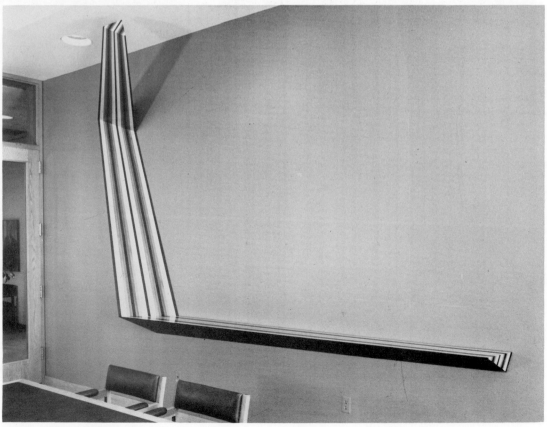

STEREO WALL CABINET. Closed and open views. Saumitra Lewis Buchner. Dao exterior with tambour doors. Alder interior. 5' wide. Photograph, Schopplein Studios

DINING-ROOM CABINET. Alan Friedman. Honduras mahogany. 30" high, 6½' long, 22" deep. Collection, Mr. and Mrs. Max Mahone, Marietta, Ohio. Photograph, Bob Lantz

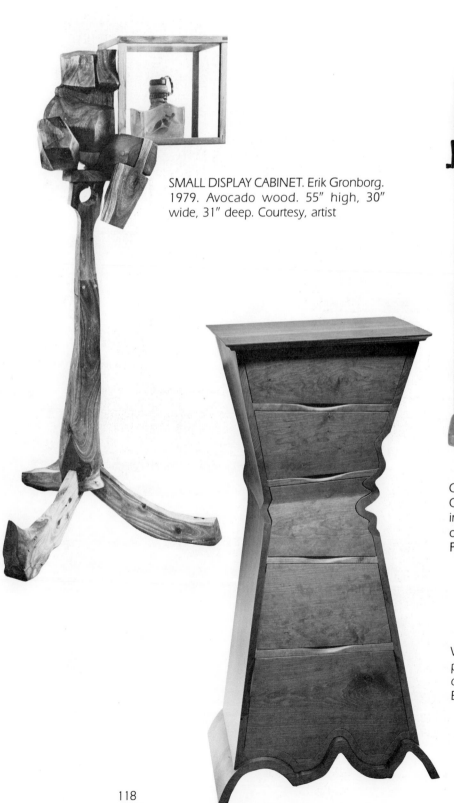

SMALL DISPLAY CABINET. Erik Gronborg. 1979. Avocado wood. 55" high, 30" wide, 31" deep. Courtesy, artist

GAS-PUMP CABINET. Fred Wall. 1978. Oak, walnut, mimosa, and copper tubing. 6½' high, 2' wide, 21" deep. Private collection. Courtesy, Works Craft Gallery, Philadelphia, PA

WOMAN. Phillip Bailey. 1975. Cherry, poplar, cedar. 53" high, 27" long, 28" deep. Collection, Elizabeth Montgomery, Beverly Hills, CA Courtesy, artist

DISPLAY CASE. Tom Brown. 1979–1980. Honduras mahogany with maple panels and curved glass front. 65" high, 20" wide, 15" deep. Photograph, Richard Sargeant

LIQUEUR CABINET. Lee Elgin. 1973. Laminated cherry with walnut inlay on doors. Marine latches and sand-cast pendant handles. 6½' high, 4' wide. Collection, I. F. Connor, Denver, CO

CABINET. John Makepeace Design and Workshop. 1980. Macassar ebony, holly, and burnished lacquer. Photograph, Jeremy Whitaker

ARMOIRE Closed and open views. Steve Voorheis. 1979. Honduras mahogany. 73"' high, 34" wide, 19" deep. A full-length mirror, which is exposed between the doors, reflects the flowing door edges along with the activity in the room, thus providing an interaction of the piece with the viewer. Within the cabinet, six shelves of different sizes have bird's-eye–maple pulls. A smaller mirror is mounted in front of two shelves above the drawers. Courtesy, artist

BELOW: QUILT STORAGE. Construction, Douglas Lowe; decoration, Mabel B. Hutchinson. 1980. The box is white birch. The decorative elements are teak, walnut, koa, redwood, and mahogany. The lid back and legs are teak. 21" high, 64" long, 19" wide. Photograph, Ardythe Smetona

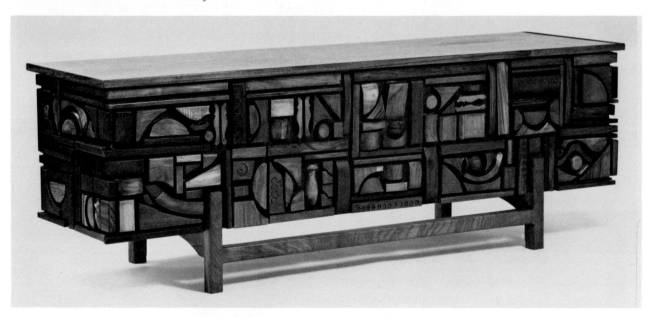

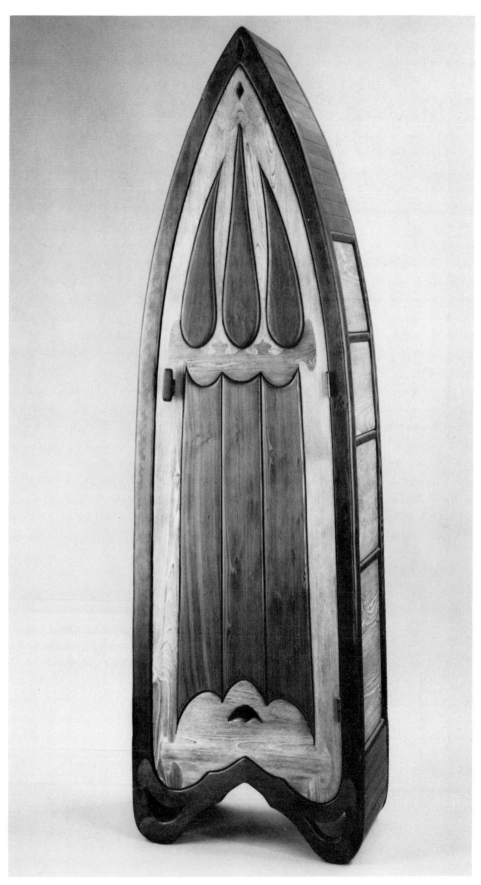

KHARTOUM. Gary Sylvester. 1979. Redwood framework.
Select pine door frame and side panels. 71" high, 22" wide,
12½" deep. Photograph, Dwight Caswell

BEDROOM SUITE. Sterling King. 1978–1979. Oak. Bed, standing mirror, dresser and blanket box with cedar lining. Bed: 60″ high, 66″ wide, 96″ deep. Dresser: 60″ high, 56″ wide, 32″ deep. Blanket box: 31″ high, 48″ wide, 21″ deep. Mirror: 72″ high, 32″ wide, 30″ deep. Collection and photograph courtesy, artist

BED FRAME. Gary Galbraith. 1979. Bent wood of oak and walnut. 82" high, 78" wide, 108" deep. Courtesy, artist

HALL TREE. Gary Galbraith. 1976. Laminated oak and walnut, compound curves of ash. Hinged storage seat, wood coat hooks, leaded mirror. 74" high, 40" wide, 18" deep. Courtesy, artist

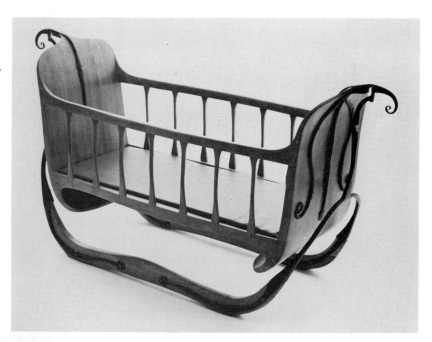

CLARK'S CRADLE. Jim Wallace. 1977. Cherry, mild steel forged. 36" high, 40" long, 22" wide. Collection, Mr. and Mrs. Ralph Clark, Jr. Crested Butte, CO. Courtesy, artist

CONTAINER FOR RECORD ALBUMS. Mark S. Levin. Walnut and oak. 32" high, 26" wide, 14" deep. Courtesy, artist

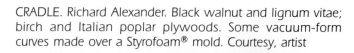

CRADLE. Richard Alexander. Black walnut and lignum vitae; birch and Italian poplar plywoods. Some vacuum-form curves made over a Styrofoam® mold. Courtesy, artist

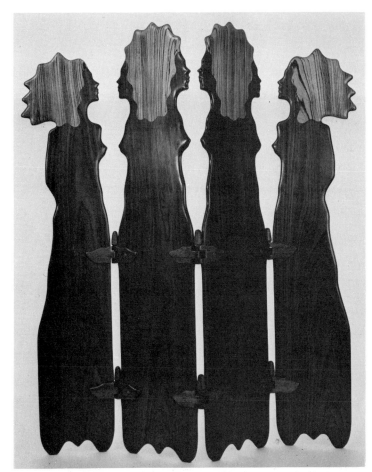

LADY SCREEN. Bobby Reed Falwell. Padouk and zebrawood. 72" high, 64" long, 1½" deep. Courtesy, artist

COAT AND HAT RACK. Jon Brooks. White pine and oak. 5' high, 2' wide. Photograph, Mark Lindquist

PLANT STAND. Mitchell Azoff. Oak, steam bent. 36" high, 11" wide, 9" deep. Courtesy, artist

HALL TREE. Frank E. Cummings. 1979. Oak, ebony, ivory, etched mirror. 79" high, 44" wide, 22" deep. Courtesy, artist

BELOW, LEFT: VALET. Bobby Reed Falwell. Red oak. 52" high, 18" wide, 20" deep. Courtesy, artist

BELOW, RIGHT: VALET. Federico Armijo. Walnut, rosewood and ebony. 72" high, 60" wide, 30" deep. Courtesy, artist

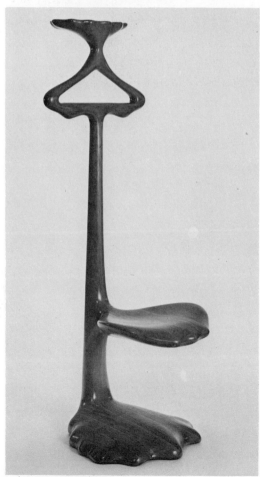

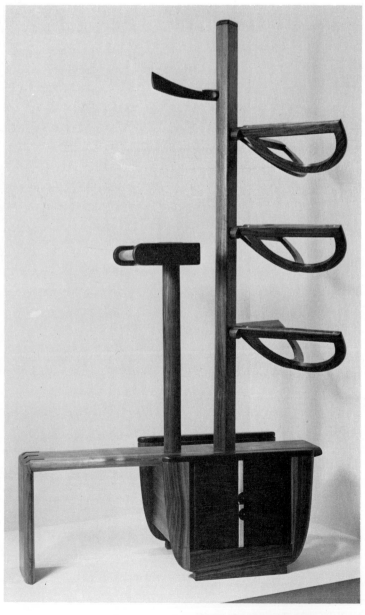

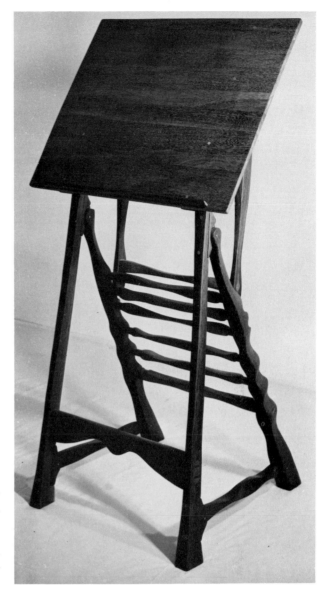

DRAWING TABLE FOR IRINA. Erik Gronborg. Avocado wood. Adjustable top surface; rungs turn for foot massage and also serve to support the table-top hinge device at different heights. 43" high, 28" wide, 28" deep. Courtesy, artist

BELOW, LEFT: FOOTSTOOL FOR GUITARIST. Lyle Laske. 1976. Rosewood. 4" high, 13" long, 8½" wide. Courtesy, artist

BELOW, RIGHT: SWING. Mitchell Azoff. Cherry. 9" high, 30" wide, 13" deep. Photograph, William Lemke

CLOCK. Frank E. Cummings. 1979–1980. Ebony case with hand-carved ivory and African black wood gears. 68" high, 24" wide, 16" deep. Cummings refers to his clock as the ultimate in kinetic sculpture. All ivory parts were developed from an original paper design of snowflakes and seapods. The paper was glued to the ivory and then all ivory parts carved. BELOW: detail. Photographs, Kenneth Naversen

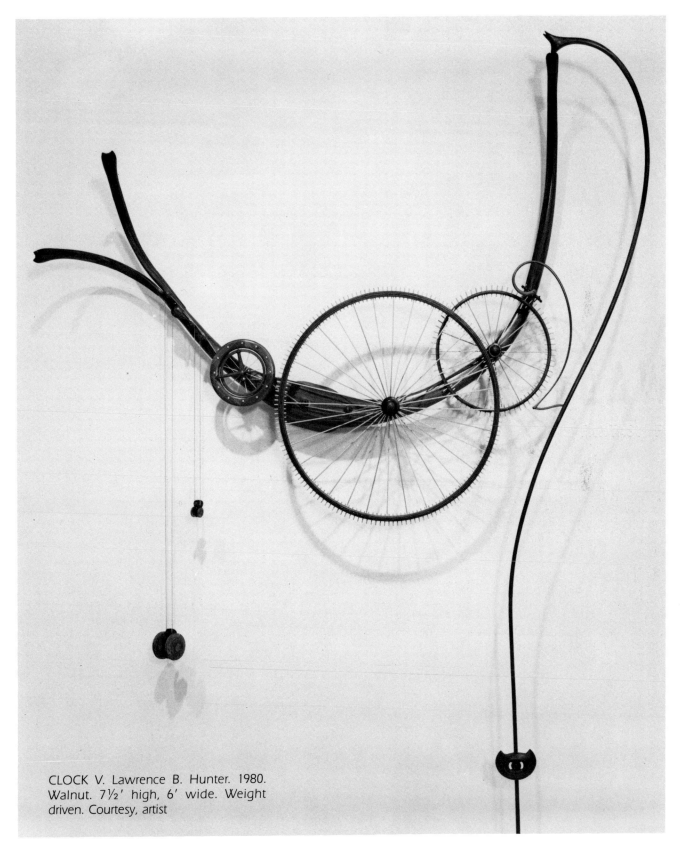

CLOCK V. Lawrence B. Hunter. 1980.
Walnut. 7½' high, 6' wide. Weight
driven. Courtesy, artist

TWO INTERIORS. Albert Garvey. ABOVE: Kitchen with cabinetry, assorted custom features. Old, rough-sawn redwood was worked with a disc sander with 50-grain paper. Laminated plywood lights. Custom tiles.

BELOW: Bathroom and shower. The artist conceived and executed all the woodwork and stone work. The door is redwood and cedar mosaic. Vanity, toilet enclosure and walls are western red cedar. Koa is used for the "tree" form, mirror frames and medicine chest. Home of Mr. and Mrs. Steven Hopper, San Rafael, CA. Photographs: courtesy, artist

707 JET INTERIOR. Paul Runge. Dividers and table. Detail of one of several various fold-down and tuck-away dining tables, cocktail tables, end tables, partitions and other appointments for the custom interior of private airplanes. For this client, the work was a blend of contemporary cabinetry accomplished in traditional design. Courtesy, artist

BANNISTER. Saswathan Quinn. Laminated cherry and shedua assembled with screws and splines. The commission was to have the bannister design tie in with the stained-glass window developed from a Henri Matisse painting. Courtesy, artist

SILO STAIRS AND BANNISTER. Andrew J. Willner. Red oak, forged iron. 14' high. Private collection, Dalton, PA

ALTAR WITH CROSS, CANDLESTICKS, PULPIT AND LECTERN.
Bill Keyser. 1977. Red-oak plywood and solid red-oak edging
over pine ribs. Sweeping vertical and/or angled planes sup-
port a horizontal surface. Lectern: Bill Keyser. 1977. Red oak.
All are installed in the Risen Christ Lutheran Church, Perinton,
NY. Photographs, Robert Kushner

132

PULPIT AND CROSS. Steve Loar. 1979. Cherry. Pulpit: 52" high,
38" wide, 38" deep. Cross: 66" high, 35" wide, 14" deep.
Prototypes for church commissions. Courtesy, artist

ALTAR RAIL. Joseph A. Agate and Fred Wildnauer. Portion of installation at First United Methodist Church, Springfield, Illinois. The rail is red oak that consists of battens 1¼″ by 6″ by 36″ that spread around a circle of a 26-foot radius. A full-scale Styrofoam® model was carved and used as a template for the final carving. After the entire piece was carved as a solid entity it was sliced, and then every other batten was removed and placed in order on the other side of the rail (the pieces were not simply spread apart). The entire project included coordinated lectern, altar, baptismal font, tables and chairs. BELOW: Detail. Photographs, Agate/Wildnauer

PART III
SCULPTURE

6

The Object as Sculpture

Only in the twentieth century has the abstract, nonobjective sculpture come into being. Before then, one had a good idea of the subject matter explored by sculptors. Themes normally encompassed human figures, animals and plant forms. Some artists strove to make the art as real as the original; others aimed for an idealism or expressionism based on their unique perceptions and abilities to transform subject into selected material.

Traditional concepts of what art is, how it should be created and what it should consist of have been shattered in the twentieth century, so that such contemplation is dizzying and refreshing. The purpose of this book is not to present a historical overview. That has been accomplished in myriad volumes to which you can refer for background.

Certainly what emerges, with any peek into the past and present art activity, is that today's artist has many more choices of materials, combinations of them, subject matter and freedom of form than did his predecessors. Wood is only one of the myriad choices the sculptor has today and it can be developed in greater variety than in the past, too, thanks to the use of motorized equipment.

The premise of this book was to exhibit the work of artists who are creating new statements, choosing wood as their medium, and to show the multiple directions in which the medium is speeding. Some artists are well known, and their present work illustrates departures from earlier statements. Other artists are emerging and establishing reputations because of their ability to express fresh ideas competently and convincingly.

How do artists develop these new statements? None of their techniques is necessarily inventive, though many have found shortcuts and solutions to their individual creative problems. I have listened patiently, and frequently, to each person who confides that he or she is the "only one" or "the first one" to use a chain saw, or a certain "innovation" to do a specific job. I smile inwardly for I may have just interviewed another artist who is doing the same thing in almost the same way with the same tool. Artists tend to work in isolation physically and mentally. They do not visit other studios to see what their peers are doing. Some adamantly avoid art publications so they are not "influenced by the ideas of others."

136

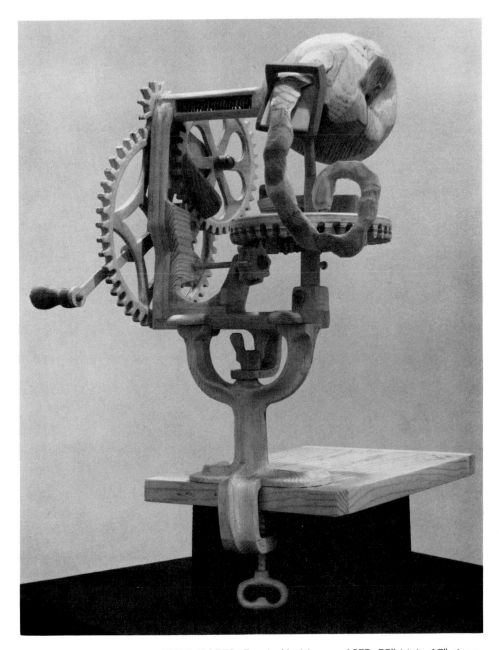

APPLE CORER. Fumio Yoshimura. 1972. 22" high, 17" deep, 17" wide. Linden, pine; the apple peel is redwood. Collection, Edward Bernstein, Philadelphia, PA. Photograph, Chie Nishio

But ideas are in the air for everyone to tune into, even subconsciously. All power tools are readily available and their potentials recognized. Whether one sculptor works from a No. 1 to a No. 600 sandpaper or a No. 200 to a No. 400 is not the essence anymore. There is ample technical information for anyone to find, absorb and apply to his needs.

What the artist does with those tools and techniques is the ultimate concern. How does he visualize his personal imagery? What does he create from the wood with which he works?

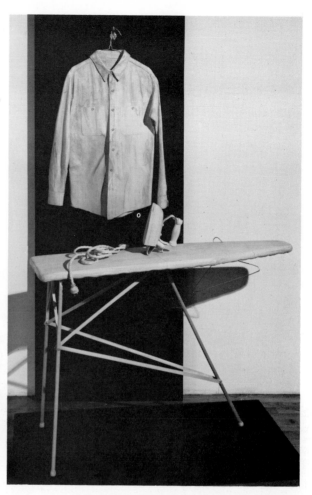

SHOPPING CART. Fumio Yoshimura. 1976. Linden wood. Actual size. Courtesy, artist

SHIRT WITH IRONING BOARD. Fumio Yoshimura. 1978. Linden wood. 79" high, 48" wide, 35" deep. Courtesy, Nancy Hoffman Gallery, New York. Photograph, Bevan Davies

Among the newest forms that emerged in profusion were recognizable everyday objects interpreted in a variety of woods. Several such objects are illustrated as furniture in Chapter 3, but "object makers," as they have already been dubbed, are using them as subjects for sculptural expression.

Why would one want to re-create familiar items such as bicycles, can openers, toasters, beer cans, pies and tools in another medium and consider it sculpture? Why not? Why are such objects any different from a body, a flower or an animal? There are as many reasons as there are artists who make them.

As an art movement, which it appears to be, the creation of real objects in wood, or in other media such as marble or metal, has a basis in reality. They are seen as objects for the study of a still life as much as is a vase or an apple. But the woodworker has another ethic from which to draw. The Japanese and Early American tool makers carved handles for tools and made beautiful cases to hold them. It was one more thought process to observe these carved objects and to make them more precious; to think of them now as sculptural objects and as nonfunctional pieces because we no longer require them to be useful. Functional objects have moved into the realm of nonfunction. Once again, the concepts of art and craft merge. How can they be denied as coexisting? How can they be sharply categorized?

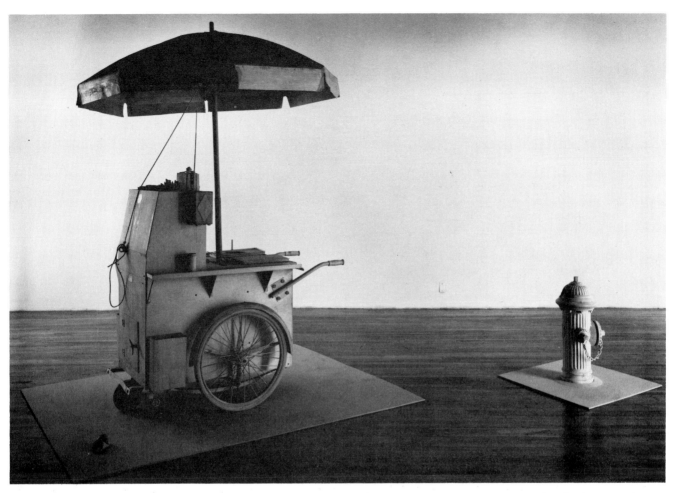

HOT-DOG CART. Fumio Yoshimura. 1979. Linden wood and poplar. Cart: 102″ high, 62″ wide, 62″ deep. Hydrant: 31½″ high, 13″ wide, 13″ deep. Courtesy, Nancy Hoffman Gallery, New York Photograph, Bevan Davies

Fumio Yoshimura explains that he does not attempt to duplicate the objects that inspire his superrealistic sculptures. He thinks of them as "the ghosts of the original objects." He takes great artistic license in interpreting the designs loosely in wood. "I extract the structure, the essence, of the object."

It is a joy to follow the development of one of Fumio's ideas from quick sketch to detailed drawing to the three-dimensional statement. He assembles the tiny hand-carved linden-wood pieces to simulate the bony fish skeleton much as one would assemble the ribs for a model airplane. The work is exacting, slow; each piece is carved with the simplest hand tools from Eastern and Western cultures and with only minimal use of power tools.

Generally, artists are unconcerned with labels such as superrealism or photorealism. They shrug their shoulders at criticism that suggests they make objects because they cannot think of anything else to create. If they wish to observe, poke fun at or be serious about society, it is their prerogative. They philosophize and observe that the "game" is to see common things developed in uncommon materials. The change of scale of an object catapults it into a different visual perspective, permitting a new awareness of the objects's shape and the relationship of its parts.

The "heritage" of this viewpoint is the early wood sculptures by H. C.

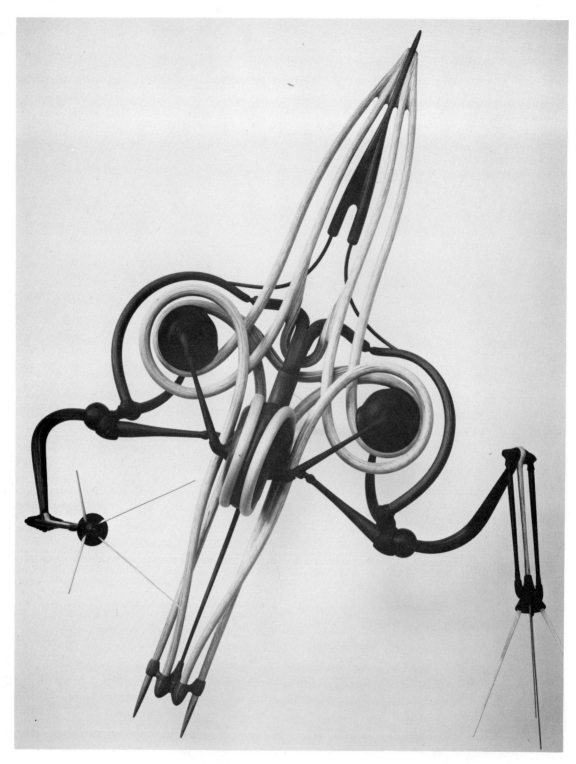

UNTITLED. Michael Cooper. 1980. Laminated hardwoods. 96" long, 68" wide, 48" deep. Ash, mansonia, teak, rosewood, vermilion, mahogany, tanzania, and birch. Collection, San Jose State University, CA. Photograph, Morley Baer

Westermann in hard materials and the subsequent expression by Claes Oldenburg of objects in soft materials. Now the artist is continuing to pioneer and explore these ideas; to see where they will lead. Only time will tell.

Perhaps there is the answer to the "why they do it" question. Each piece leads an artist to observe a new facet of an object in another way. It poses

Detail of UNTITLED (OPPOSITE). Michael Cooper. Photograph, Oscar Savio

additional avenues to travel. Unless they proceed, unless they create, unless they grow and mature in their ideas, they will never push on to newer visions, newer adventures, newer discoveries. That is the perpetual carrot, always fresh and enticing, held at the end of the artistic wand.

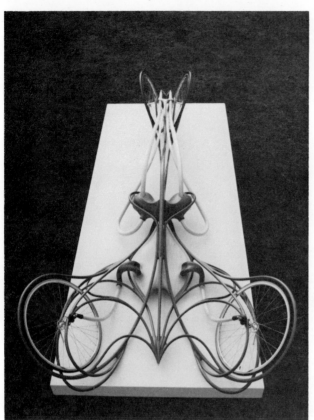
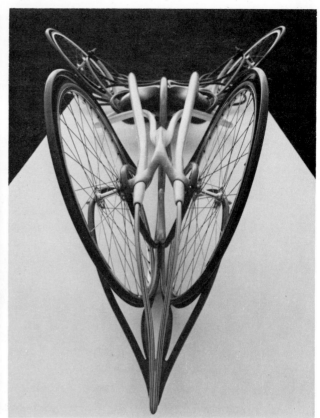

DUNLOP. Michael Cooper. 1979. Three views. Laminated Australian timbers—Queensland silver ash, Tasmanian blackwood, blue gum, red oak, black bean. 148" long, 28" high, 68" wide. Photographs, Bob Heidrich

LOADED WITH EXTRAS. Michael Cooper. 1979. Two views.
Laminated Australian jarrah. 41″ long, 25″ high, 28″ wide.
Photographs, R. J. Muna

SCOOTER SEVEN. Kurt Widstrand. 1975. Bent and laminated walnut with cocobolo, rosewood and ironwood insets. 34" high, 78" long, 26" wide. The piece is functional: it has a working caliper brake in the rear wheel housing. Collection, City of Palo Alto, CA. Photograph, Russ Widstrand

LEFT: BOUNCING BETTY. Kurt Widstrand. 1977. Laminated and bent walnut and zebrawood, nylon, anodized aluminum wheels, black zinc steel. 27" high, 104" long, 16" wide. It will freewheel downhill with a rider in a prone position supported by the nylon and fins. Brakes in the rear are activated by a level in the handle; a cable to the brake is buried between the laminations. Photograph, Russ Widstrand

OPPOSITE: CROQUET SETS. Timothy P. Curtis.

A surrealistic adaptation of the concept of the croquet set is constructed on an enlarged scale. Each mallet, cart and ball explores the graceful, continuous movement in the forms. The functional aspects of the game do not dictate the design.

Each mallet is designed to stimulate and arouse the viewer to become physically involved while attempting to recapture a quality of a childhood experience—that of playing croquet. The artist's springboard was his own remembrance of playing the game with mallets too large to handle, oversized balls, wire hoops to trip over, and the grown-ups' drinks to spill. This was coupled with the myriad detailed and ritualistic aspects of the game played more seriously as an adult.

The results of all the remembered stimulae and the need to express the idea sculpturally are intricately and rhythmically developed in laminated and bent wood.

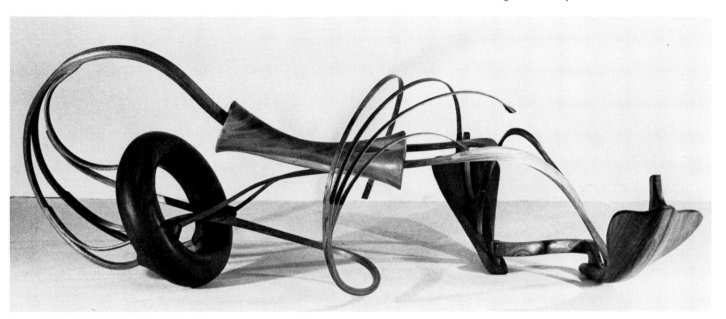

CROQUET SET. Timothy P. Curtis. 1979. Hardwoods. 5' high,
15' long, 9' wide. Courtesy, artist

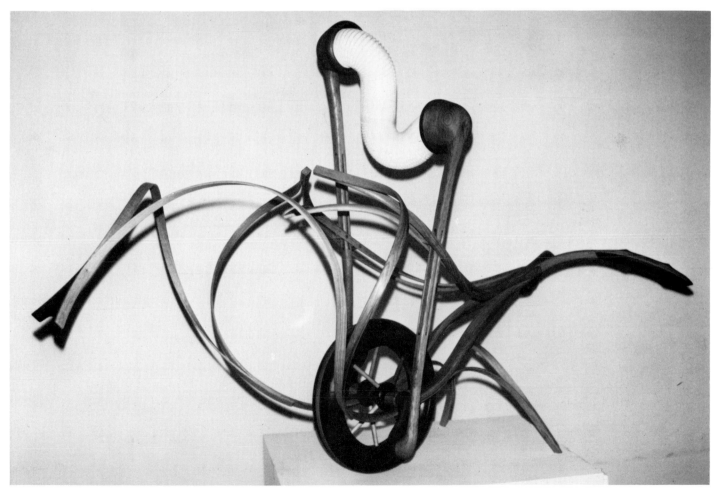

CROQUET SET. Timothy P. Curtis. 1979. Hardwoods. 5' high,
6' long, 2' wide. Courtesy, artist

TOOTH SAW. David King. 1963. Hickory, sugar pine, steel, human teeth. 8" high, 36" long, 10" deep. Collection, Dr. Gary Staycart, Pt. Richmond, CA

HAMMOWER. David King. 1975. Walnut with inlaid walnut and maple dowels. 8" high, 14" wide, 20" deep. Collection, Ebin Haskill, Sacramento, CA. All photographs courtesy, Hank Baum Gallery, San Francisco, CA

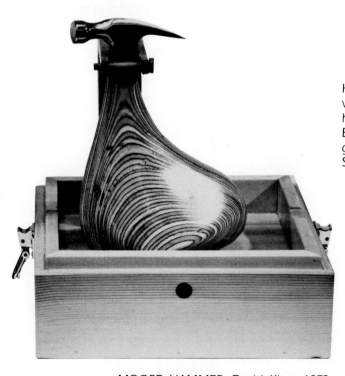

MOORE HAMMER. David King. 1973. Laminated birch, sugar pine, silver-plated metal hammer head. 22" high, 14" square (box cover not shown).

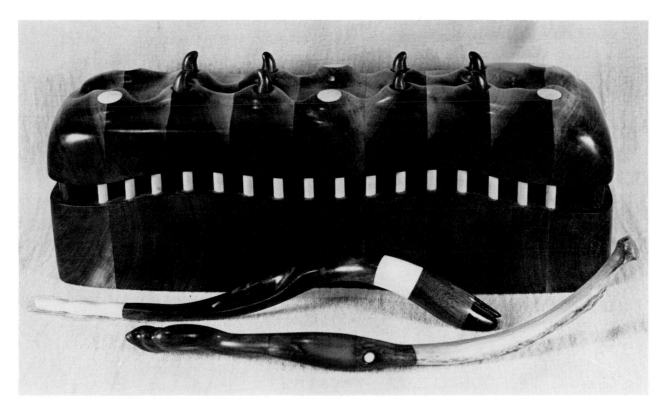

SACRARIUM FOR SEQUESTERED POWER OBJECTS. Don Schule. Walnut, bone, antler, deer hoof, fur. 14" long.

"Most of my sculpture is composed of an interior piece, which is the heart of the work and is to be handled, and a container that serves to house it. In this way, the nugget of the work is hidden and protected and does not lose its power through overexposure, and therefore, overfamiliarity. The seminal influences for my work are Zen meditation, Tae Kwon Do and love of nature."

Don Schule

DOVETAILED SACRARIUM. Don Schule. Walnut and bone. 9" long.

CONJURE BONE. Don Schule. Walnut, bone, bronze and leather. 13" long. All photographs courtesy, artist

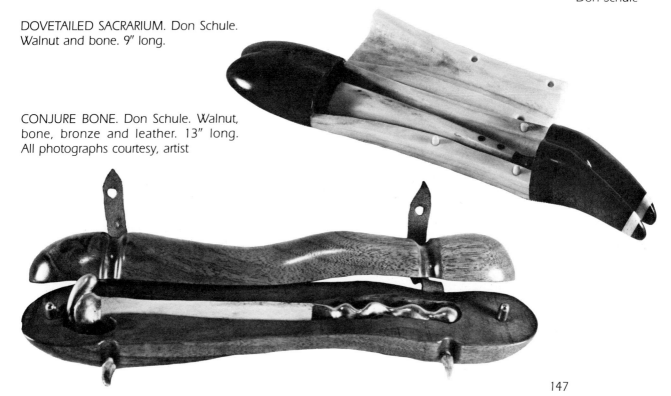

147

BAMBOO 1. Dennis Morinaka. 1980. New Guinea walnut, square Japanese bamboo, maple, osage orange, brass, leather. 66" long, 7½" high, 10½" deep. Closed and open views, and interior piece of bamboo. Courtesy, artist

"The essence of what I am doing is making 'cases' for 'cases.' I have made or constructed everything including the brass catches on the front. I became interested in the concept as a result of seeing pictures of square bamboo."
Dennis Morinaka

BAMBOO 2. Dennis Morinaka. 1980. Eastern maple. Round Japanese bamboo, rosewood, brass, leather. 6¾" high, 41" long, 9½" deep. TOP: Closed. BELOW: Open with bamboo cut in half. Courtesy, artist

148

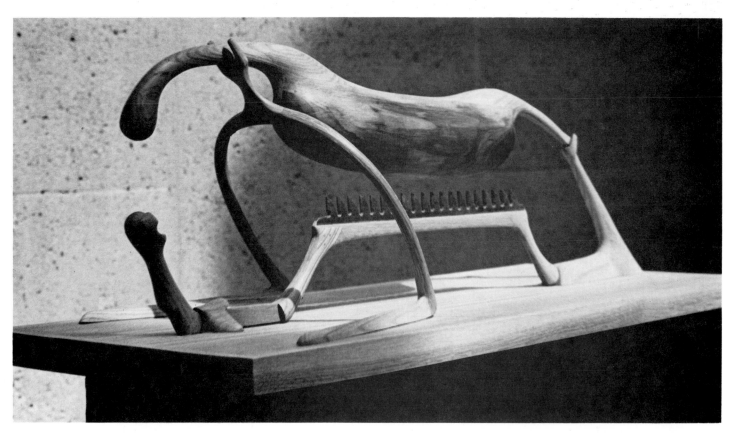

SAWHORSE. Morse Clary. White oak, red oak, walnut, and purpleheart. 48" long, 21" high, 21" deep. This is a kinetic sculpture; the saw slides on a track and the topmost form pivots on a dowel and moves up and down. The movement enables the viewer to take an active part in the change as the forms move in relation to one another and to space. Courtesy, artist

METROROCKER. Ralph Johnson. 1977. Wood and mechanical movements. 27" high, 9" wide, 19" deep. Courtesy, Hank Baum Gallery, San Francisco

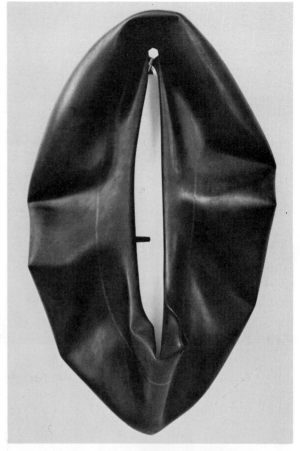

HELLO, DOLLY! Robert Bourdon. 1980. Life size. Mixed woods. Photograph, D. James Dee

TOP RIGHT: MAJOR MINOR'S SMILE IS FINER. Robert Bourdon. August 1978. Carved and stained Honduras mahogany. Life size, about 22" high. Collection, Allan Stone, New York

TEXAS TASTE. Robert Bourdon. Fall 1976. Carved and fabricated Honduras mahogany. Life size. Collection, Ken Harris, Rapid City, SD

BUSTED FLAT. Robert Bourdon. 1980. Carved and painted Honduras mahogany. 32" high, 40" wide, 2" deep. Collection, Teddy Westreich, Washington, DC

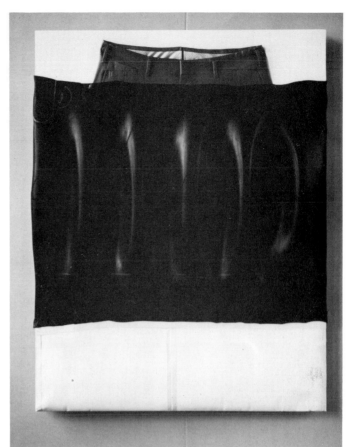

"My process is one of problem building and solving. Each piece presents a new dilemma. The solutions, in turn, create new questions. As a consequence the imagery grows ever more complex and obtuse. The main conceptual hurdle is to maintain a coherent image whose integrity is not lost in the process.

"For some problems I may work on twenty to thirty models. With luck, one will present the problems and solutions I have in mind. The actual sculptures are directly carved from solid laminated blocks of Honduras mahogany, then painted in the likeness of the model. What appears to be paper, tape, clothing, rubber and so forth, are, in reality, illusions in painted wood. I use extremely sharp tools, with intense cross light to help me create the perfect illusion I am seeking. A hospital operating table facilitates working; I am able to raise, lower and turn the wood as I need to work in various areas and directions."

Robert Bourdon

BAGGY PANTS. Robert Bourdon. 1979. Carved and painted Honduras mahogany. 40" high, 32" wide, 3" deep. Collection, Mr. and Mrs. Paul Denison, Carpenteria, CA

A RACING CARCASS BOUND FOR HOME. Robert Bourdon. 1973–1978. Three views. Wood and leather. 35" high, 216" long, 32" wide. The piece refers to the spaces of a nontechnological society within a geologic time framework. Courtesy, artist

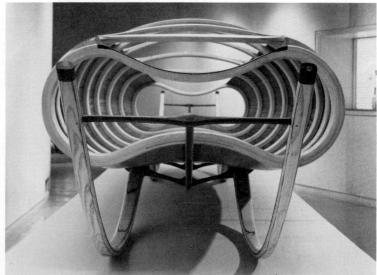

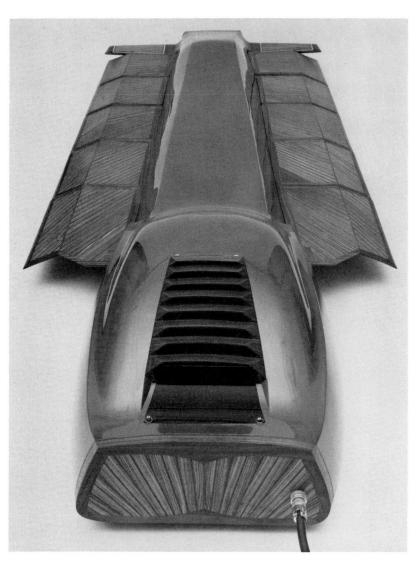

SWEET DREAMS, FANGIO. Robert Bourdon. 1980. Padouk, African mahogany, Brazilian tulip, synthetic fiberglass, epoxy paint and metal. 18" high, 126" long, 42" wide. Courtesy, artist

"This is a cybernetic sculpture incorporating an electrohydraulic power system with a Kim-1 microprocessor as the 'brains.' The piece is triggered by a series of ultrasonic transistors which determine, with the aid of the computer, the speed of movement (and to some extent the bulk) of the viewer. The sculpture, in turn, reacts to the viewer in various threatening or aggressive behavior patterns, seeming to interpret its audience rather than vice versa."

Robert Bourdon

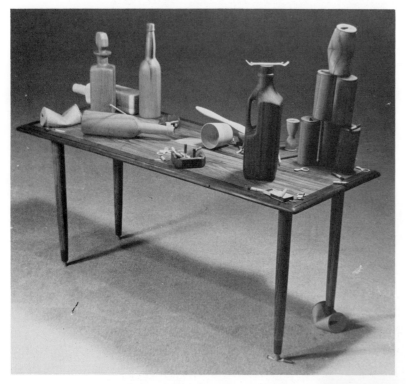

THE PARTY TABLE. John W. Mc-Naughton. 1979. Oak, walnut, cherry, elm, poplar and maple. 28" high, 48" wide, 16" deep.

BELOW, LEFT: EARLY AMERICAN TABLES LEAVE ME LIMP. John W. McNaughton. 1979. Walnut, maple, oak. 34" high, 14" square. Collection, Mrs. Edith Perlstein, Los Angeles, CA

"My work has to go beyond a nice, recognizable form. It has to be an art object which makes a statement, a message with impact. Humor and whimsy play important roles.... Usually I will use a series of sketches; often full-size sketches and models. Sometimes I use foam rubber to mold a prototype and to think through any potential problems. I always see new things as a piece develops and feel free to make subtle changes. I'm stimulated by those changes."

John W. McNaughton

THE BREAKFAST TABLE. John W. McNaughton. 1979. Oak, coffee bean, pine, walnut, cherry, maple. 40" high, 28" square. All photographs courtesy, artist

JUNE 14, 1945. THE GOLDEN URINAL CAFÉ. C. R. Johnson. 1980. Back side. Men's room. Basswood tiles with padouk border. Urinal of beech with walnut plumbing. Oak flush tank (the urinal will work with the plastic waste-basket mounted in the tank). Plastic pipes and fixtures with flush mechanism are within the walnut. The walnut radiator has a basswood pop-off valve and control lightswitch plate. Graffiti. Courtesy, artist

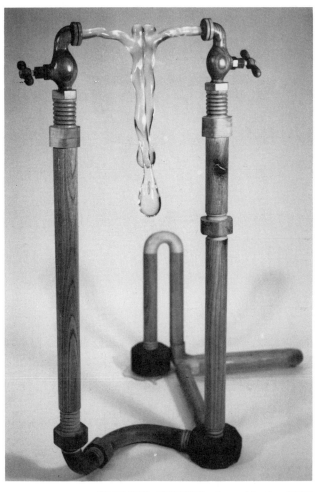

DUELING FAUCETS. Amy Musia. 1980. Laminated sassafras, pine, red and white oak, with Plexiglas® drips and puddle. Lathe turned with hand-carved faucets and bolts. 48" high, 36" wide, 24" deep. Courtesy, artist

CRUDE WOOD No. 1. Carl E. Johnson. Walnut and brass. 48" high, 24" wide at the base. Courtesy, artist

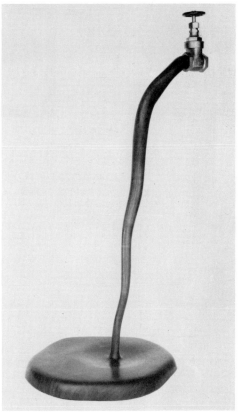

MOTH SHIRT. Bruce Guttin. 1977. Pine. 17" high, 9½" wide, 7" deep. Courtesy, artist

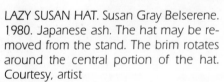

LAZY SUSAN HAT. Susan Gray Belserene. 1980. Japanese ash. The hat may be removed from the stand. The brim rotates around the central portion of the hat. Courtesy, artist

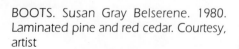

BOOTS. Susan Gray Belserene. 1980. Laminated pine and red cedar. Courtesy, artist

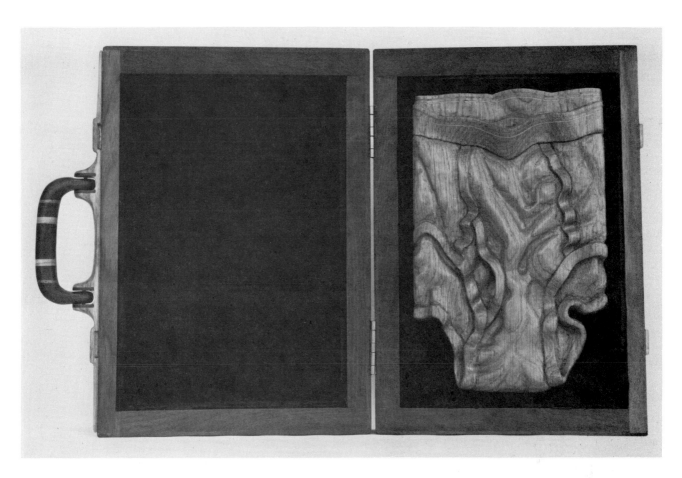

BRIEFCASE. Morse Clary. 1979. White oak, black walnut, red oak and purpleheart. ABOVE: open view; BELOW: closed view. 11" high, 15" wide, 4" deep. Courtesy, artist

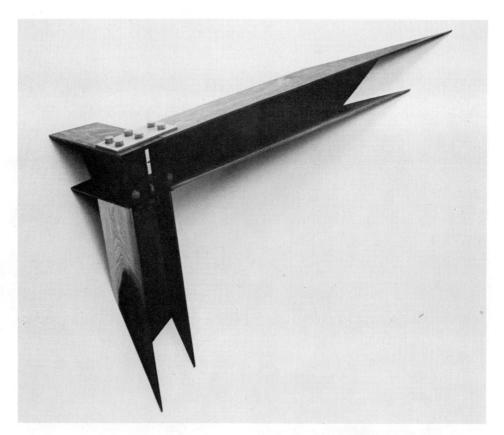

GIRDER STRUCTURE. Stephen L. Casey.
1979. Walnut, cherry, birch. 60" wide, 24"
high, 12" deep. Courtesy, artist
   "An everyday object taken out of context and made in wood is designed to
take your eye from any place on a large
wall to a central focal point."

PLUMBER'S HELPER. Ronnie J. Rogers.
1980. Walnut, hard maple, cherry, reed
and finished with oil. Courtesy, artist
   "I like to combine humor or satire into
a different way of seeing things. I often
use movement so that the viewer becomes involved with the piece."

BASEBALL MITT. Mark Lindquist. 1977. Wormy butternut. Life size. Courtesy, artist.

SARDINE CAN. Gib Taylor. Cherry, birch and walnut. 9" long, 7" wide, 3½" deep. Courtesy, artist

SLICE OF PIE. Gib Taylor. Maple and butternut. 3" high, 13" long. Courtesy, artist

STILL LIFE IN PROCESS. Caroline Gassner Kaplowitz. 1979. Carved pine and tools. 24" high, 17" wide, 17" deep.

"The still life format enables me to develop my prevailing interest in the many aspects of sculptured form ... to combine subject matter found in art, life and nature. A counterpoint is established between the objects' volumes and linear movement of the 'drape.' Other contrasts I explore as variations of form are: hard vs. soft, open vs. closed, controlled vs. spontaneous, ambiguous vs. clarified, and created vs. natural—and/or life forms."

Caroline Gassner Kaplowitz

STILL LIFE WITH SHELLS. Caroline Gassner Kaplowitz. 1979. Carved pine and shells. 11" high, 15½" wide, 16½" deep. Photographs courtesy, artist

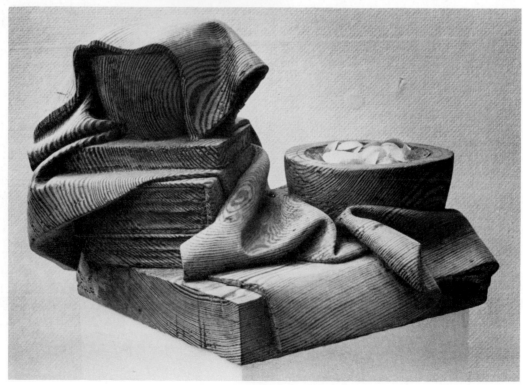

"Beginning in 1970, my work grew out of painting-on-canvas problems to become another of the current flock of hybrids between painting and sculpture. My painted plywood constructions have been primarily concerned with trompe l'oeil effects since about 1974; most of these recent pieces have used women's antique clothing as subject matter, though of late I've been getting interested in such things as leaves and sticks.

"For these works, I pin the actual object to a Styrofoam® panel and begin to analyze its three-dimensional relief structure in terms of planes which can be made of birch plywood. Some of these constructions require as many as three or four hundred pieces of wood to build. My tools are a jigsaw and a belt and disc sander; I do not carve. When completed, the wooden construction is painted realistically with acrylics, in what I would

(Continued on next page)

TWO-PIECE SWIMSUIT II. Ron Isaacs. 1979. Birch plywood construction with acrylic. The suit is life size. The sculpture overall is 41" high, 22" wide, 4½" deep. RIGHT: The construction before painting. Courtesy, artist

BATTENBERG LACE. Ron Isaacs. 1979.
Finnish birch-plywood construction with
acrylic. Life size. 27½" high, 27" wide,
2¾" deep. Collection, Mr. and Mrs. Fred
Mittleman, New York

OPPOSITE: Detail.
Each leaf form may be composed of as
many as fifteen separate pieces assembled into the necessary planes and
shapes, then polychromed. Courtesy,
artist

(Continued from preceding page)

like to think of as a painterly manner. I depend on the illusions created by the paint to carry details of the structure
which could not be translated into wood.

I enjoy the fusion and confusion of actual and painted
form in the pieces, as well as the indisputable ridiculousness
of a grown man making, say, plywood lingerie. Like most
artists, I impose a lot of silliness on myself in the name of art.

"The formal considerations of the work generally take
precedence over other kinds of content for me, but I hope
to move toward enriching the evocative power of the pieces."

Ron Isaacs

163

TOMATO PLANT WITH TOMATOES. Fumio Yoshimura. 1979. Linden wood. Life size. Photograph, Chie Nishio

SUNFLOWERS (Detail). Fumio Yoshimura. Linden wood and bamboo. Each flower of a bouquet is about 16" diameter. Photograph, Dona Mielach

SOWING THE SEED OF PROSPERITY. Robin VanLear. 1980. Packet is carved basswood, 7" high, 28" long, 21" wide. The pit is carved black walnut, 9½" long, 6" high, 7" deep. ABOVE: front of packet; BELOW: back of packet. Photographs, Jesse Rhinehart

"The packet is hollow and the halves fit together. The packet is designed to appear torn and faded. The inside is natural maple with a lacquer finish. The outside has a base coat of semitransparent oil-base stain sealed with lacquer. The images are airbrushed; the lettering is acrylic. A press-type lettering was used on the packet back and then subtly faded out with an overspray and lacquer finish.

"The peach pit, which fits in the packet, is hollow, and contains a coin-operated music box and a coin slot. It plays 'If I Were a Rich Man.'"

Robin VanLear

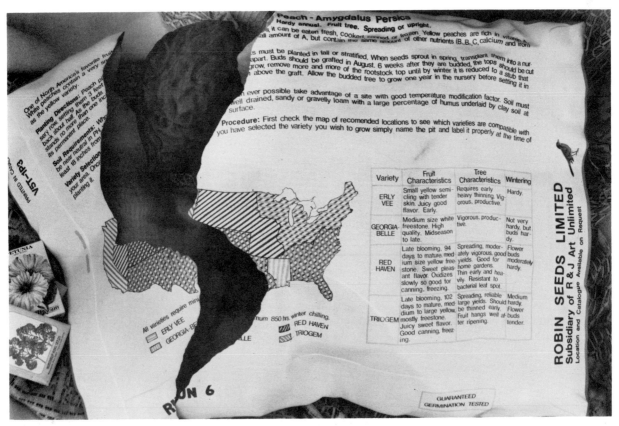

TRIPTYCH, DEDICATED TO FLANNERY O'CONNER. Tom Duncan. 1978. Wood, found objects, collage, lights, plaster, acrylic. 7'8" high, 45" wide, 19" deep. ABOVE: detail; BELOW: entire sculpture.

"My inspiration comes from a fantasy world, coupled with a background and fascination with Coney Island and circuses. Probably every important detail of my work I've directly or indirectly seen or felt on Fourteenth Street (in New York). I've always loved the clothing and costumes and paraphernalia that people do and don't wear.... I've always had a different point of view of the world and I hope to keep it even if it is very painful at times.

"When I finish a piece of sculpture I feel an incredible relief that it is done, especially a large piece. They take about two years to do, but I feel as if a part of me has died. Usually I work on a number of pieces at once so when one piece is finished, it is not difficult to continue on another."

Tom Duncan

166

. . . AND A CAST OF THOUSANDS. Robin VanLear. 1980. A Japanese oak cabinet houses found objects and a miniature diorama entombed at the top. Brass locks, keys, fittings, screening, acrylic tops on drawers, fabric and paints. Photograph, Jesse Rhinehart

UNTITLED. Tyler James Hoare. 1975. 3M color on wood applied with a dry mount transfer. The front is steam bent over a wood form. 48" high, 30" wide, 8" deep. Photograph, Dona Meilach

ADMINISTRATOR. Tyler James Hoare, 1975. Wood, metal. 60" high, 68" long, 20" deep. Collection, Oakland Museum, Oakland, CA

If a count were made of the sculpture most often noticed by the public, possibly some of the pieces created by Tyler James Hoare would be among the highest-scoring. Many are perched on pilings in the bay alongside the freeway that parallels the water's edge at Berkeley and Emeryville, California. There are figures, airplanes and boats, all of which elicit smiles and wonderment from passers-by. Tyler makes carefully carved constructed pieces, such as the Viking Ship (ABOVE), then launches it. Nature and fate invariably dash it back ashore, often in many parts. Tyler then simply recycles the parts into more sculptures. He accepts the fate of his pieces "as 'nature's way.' It's almost a game. Fun."

But Tyler has another side to his creativity which can be seen by the pieces in his studio, page 250, which is a recycled store.

VIKING SHIP. Tyler James Hoare. 1978. Wood, mixed media. 10' high, 16' long, 8' wide. Three views and three conditions. Photographs, John David Arms

AIRPLANE. Tyler James Hoare. 1976. Mixed woods, objects. Installed on a piling in Berkeley shore, San Francisco Bay, California. 12' long, 12-foot wingspan. Courtesy, artist

BIPLANE. Tyler James Hoare. 1978. Wood, objects. Polychromed. 14' long, 12' wide, 6' high. From "On the Go" Exhibit, Fine Arts Museum of San Francisco. Photograph, John David Adams

When a plane doesn't fly or walk, it escalates for its installation journey at San Francisco's Embarcadero Center. This is one of the myriad problems that must be solved by sculptors. At rear, Tyler James Hoare. Photograph, John David Adams

7

The Figure

It is amazing to think about the changes made by artists in their interpretations of the human figure through the centuries while the general shape of the figure remains constant. From the earliest known sculptural form of the body, "The Venus of Willendorf," ca. 15,000 to 10,000 B.C., through the Greek, Roman, Renaissance, Impressionist, Post-Impressionist and the twentieth century periods, the changes can be fitted across the brain in a moment. Consider how the body was portrayed and changed from Phidias to Michelangelo, to Rodin, to Brancusi, to Giacometti and Moore. Given the same torso and limbs to deal with, the variety is infinite.

Probably every artist who attempted to interpret the body felt his imagery was unique. Yet some have been much more distinctive than others. In our generation, probably Henry Moore exerted the greatest influence on figurative sculpture through the reapportioning of the body's parts one to another as he saw and captured new relationships of space and distance.

Regardless of the form given the body by today's sculptors, the expressive ideas that emanate from the sculpture are often the surfboard on which the figure is launched into The New Wave. In the hands of people like C. Regina Kelley and Margerey Eleme Goldberg, the pieces become a strong statement of the attitude of today's woman. Their figures have a presence; the subjects are strong and powerful; they almost have a voice that reverberates with the struggles of all women before and in the present.

Barbara Spring works wood with such brilliant tactile and visual qualities that the results appear not as "wood." Rather, the figures appear to have real skin, real clothing, and they exist in a stage setting. Intellectually we know they are unreal, yet visually they take on nearly human characteristics. We look at them and recognize in them people we have met. We tend to imbue them with characteristics we think they could possess, based on our own experiences. The result is a presence, almost a reality, and there is boundless variety from every viewpoint, every nuance, every inch of the woods' grain, color and texture.

Artists whose experiences are deeply rooted in realism or in the abstractions of sculptures of the past two or three decades are beginning to break from these familiar shapes and to explore a new expressionism for the figure. Their

ANNABELL AND MISS GOODENOUGH. Barbara Spring. 1976. Various woods, with the dress made of resin and madrone chips inlaid and polished to create the floral pattern. The entire scene is life size and measures 15 feet by 18 feet. All objects and figures are carved of woods of varying colors. Photograph, Richard Sargent

pieces try to capture a soul within that cries out for identity as a being: the beautifully articulated sculptural form is not the only ideal or justification for its existence.

The artist's environment exerts a force that is evident in some pieces. John Boomer's sculptures emerge from his association and background with the American Indian. Though born on the West Coast in an urban society, he has lived on a northern New Mexico Indian reservation for many years.

Animals, fish and birds, always popular subjects among artists, continue to provide inspiration, and several examples are shown.

CITY INSPECTOR. Barbara Spring. May 1976. Life size. All figures and objects are wood. The inspector's dressing gown is
fiberglass with sawdust added to create the terry-cloth texture. The "tiles" are wood, stained white to gray; they are
loose and must be fitted together each time the sculpture is
exhibited. Photograph, Richard Sargent

ANNABELL'S AUNT. Barbara Spring. 1978. Redwood. 30 inches high, 19" wide, 17" deep. Chain-saw carved from one piece of redwood. Fine sanding produces a difference in texture between the face and the rough-sawn hair. The beads are separate. Photograph, Richard Sargent

PATIENCE CUTTING. Barbara Spring. 1980. Arms, head and legs are cypress. The dress pattern is made of ¼-inch-thick olive and avocado chip cuttings from last year's trees inlaid into resin. 5'5" high. Photograph, Lee Fatherree

HEADACHE. Barbara Spring. 1971. Redwood head and hair. Alaskan cedar scarf. The dress pattern is made from sliced pine cones inlaid and sanded smooth. 36" high. Courtesy, artist

BOXED IN. Wolfgang Behl. 1979. Cherry. 40" high, 12" wide.

PERSEPHONE. Wolfgang Behl. 1979. Cherry and oak. 62" high, 58" wide. Photographs, E. Irving Blomstrann

PIERCED RELIEF. C. Regina Kelley. 1980. 12″ high, 5½″ wide, 2″ deep. Courtesy, artist

MICHELLE AND FRIENDS. R. H. Karol. 1979–1980. Contour sculptures in a variety of hard woods including walnut, cherry, red oak, mahogany, rosewood, teak and zebrawood. Finished sculptures may vary from 12 inches to life size.

VACATION. R. H. Karol. 1980. Life size. Observe the varying directions of the woods to accomplish the contouring. Courtesy, Jeri Galleries, Marlboro, NJ. Photographs, Victor Pustai

DEEP-DISH WHEELBARROW. Doug Freerksen. 1979. White pine. 30" high, 72" long, 28" wide. Courtesy, artist

OBJECT I (Woman as Object Series). Richard Hoptner. Teak. 8" high, 36" long, 8" deep. Courtesy, artist

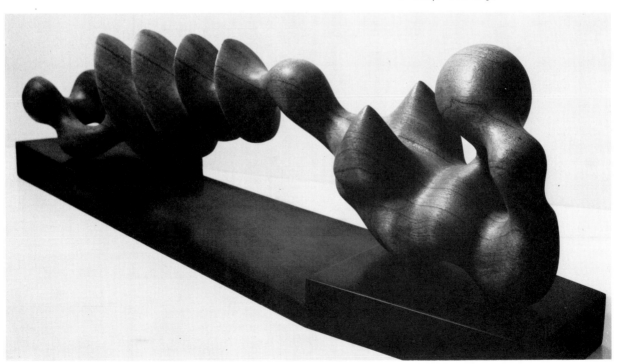

177

Woodworking: The New Wave

INITIAL POINT. Richard Hoptner. 1980.
Mahogany. 20" high, 12" wide, 10" deep.
Photograph, Rick Echelmeyer

I'M LOSING MY MIND. Margery Eleme
Goldberg. 1979. Cherry and acrylic. 5'
high. Courtesy, artist

THE FAMILY. Margery Eleme Goldberg.
1978. Thirteen different exotic woods. 17"
high., Courtesy, artist

178

LEFT: WHITE ORCHID. John Boomer. 1980. Walnut. 20" high, 10" wide, 3" deep.

TWO WOMEN. John Boomer. 1980. Walnut. 18" high, 9" wide, 4" deep. Photographs, Peter L. Bloomer

NUCLEAR FAMILY, CONTROLLED FIS-
SION. Frank Smullin. 1978. Oak. Chain-
saw carved. 56" high, 39" wide, 33" deep.
Courtesy, artist

HOMO SAPIENS II. Joshua Hoffman.
1979. Catalpa, butternut. 8' high, 4' wide,
1' deep. Courtesy, artist

VISAGES DE MON VISAGE. Jephan de
Villiers. 1979. Wooden boxes blackened
with candle smoke containing seven figures made of pieces of wood found in
the forest, autumn leaves and feathers.
Faces are made of treated bread crumbs.
13" high, 6" wide, 3½" deep. Courtesy,
artist

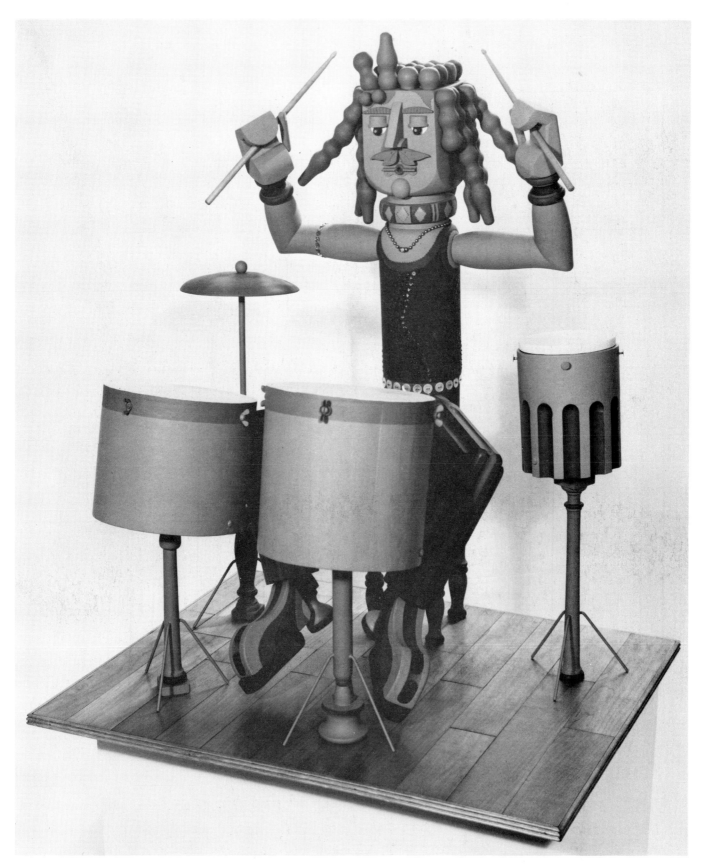

SIR CHARLES MEADE OF THE BAND "CHUMBI." *Jacqueline Fogel. 1979. Polychromed wood. 36" high, 30" wide, 24" deep. One of a series of contemporary musicians. Photograph, Sheldon Rose*

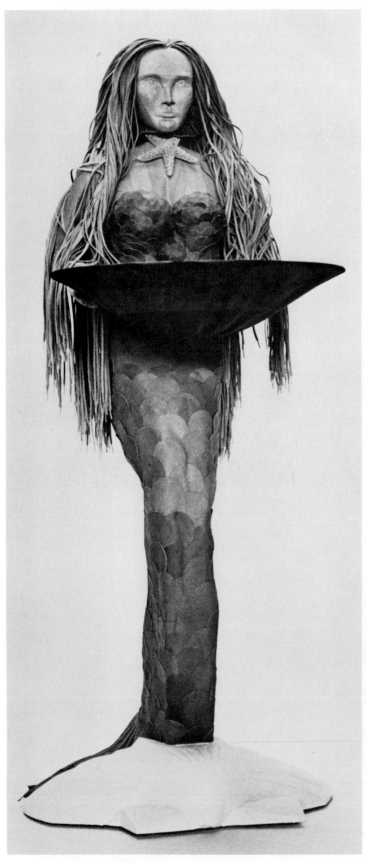

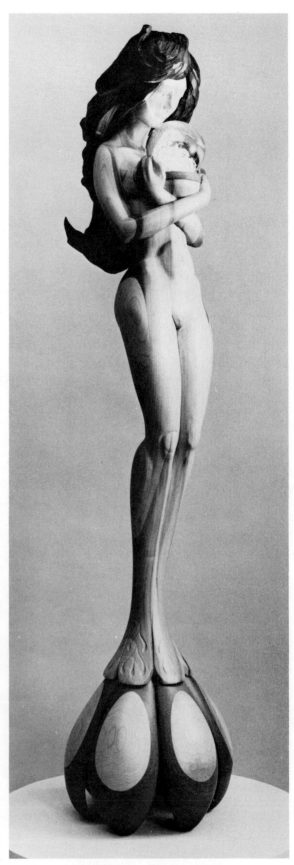

MERMAID #1. Neal M. Widett. Pine, on "shell" of pine painted white. Her scales are green leather; her hair is tan shoelaces; the shell she is holding is laminated Honduras mahogany. 68" high, 25" wide, 34" deep. Courtesy, artist

FLORA. Jeffrey Briggs. 1980. Poplar with walnut hair and a mahogany and poplar lily base from which she is emerging. She holds a hand-blown glass ball by Robert Stephan. 54" high. Collection, Mr. and Mrs. Lewis Benatar, Brewster, NY Photograph, John Russell

BARFLY (LEFT) and STREETWALKER (RIGHT). Allan Fougner. 1979. Hand-carved basswood. Approximately 10" high and 11" high. Photographs, Dona Meilach

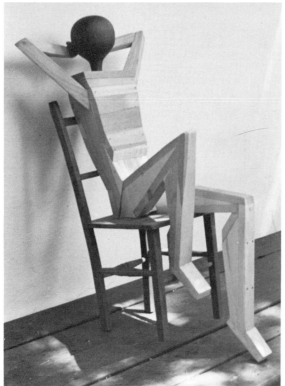

KICKING BACK. Ronald S. Moore. 1979. Pine body, black walnut head. 27" high, 18" wide, 22" deep. Courtesy, artist

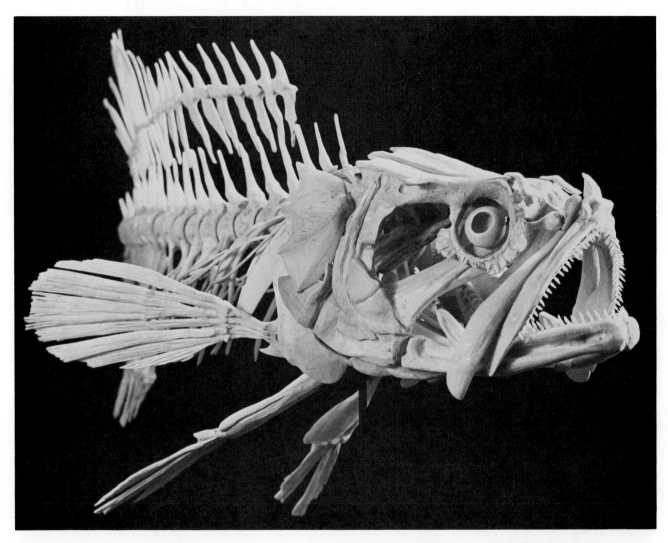

GROUPER. Fumio Yoshimura. 1976. Linden. 58" long. Collection, Norton Gallery of Art, West Palm Beach, FL. Photograph, Hiro Ihara

MANTA. Robert Ewing. 1980. Laminated Sugar Pine. 30" high.
Courtesy, artist

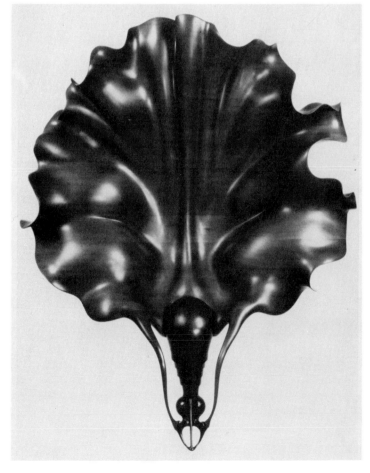

DREAMER. Peter Robbie. 1976. Two views. Honduras mahogany, padouk, purpleheart. 48" high, 39" wide, 12" deep. Courtesy, artist

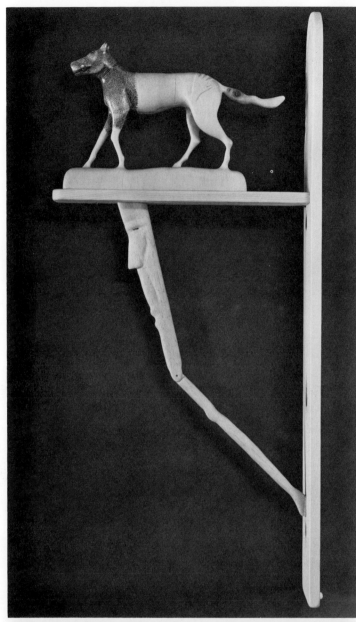

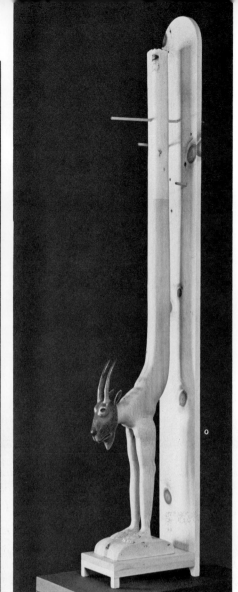

SCAPEGOAT. Michael K. Stevens. 1980. Pine, enamel and metal. 63" high, 15" wide, 7" deep.

THE THIN MAN'S PILLAR. Michael K. Stevens. 1979. Pine and enamel. 40" high, 18" wide, 5" deep.

"I have worked with 'found' limbs and wood (pine) since 1968. I use wood as a vehicle to carve out my visual concerns. The properties of wood that are attractive to me are the flaws, grains, wrinkles, cracks, stretch marks, pits and pimples—characteristics that closely resemble human skin.

"I approach my sculpture in a visual 'narrative manner.' Each piece is a story containing various images, based on a 'personal alphabet.'"

Michael K. Stevens

STEED. Michael K. Stevens. 1980. Pine and enamel. 36" high, 39" wide, 5½" deep. All photographs, Kurt E. Fishback

186

FLIGHT 67 BIRTHBIRD. Berthold J. Schmutzhart. Basswood, walnut, birch and steel. 62" high.

MIDDLE: FLIGHT 53 CARRIER. Berthold J. Schmutzhart. Poplar, walnut, epoxy resin and steel. 66" high.

BOTTOM: FLIGHT 55 FEMALE SUBMARINE. Berthold J. Schmutzhart. Walnut and steel. 44" long. All photographs, Conroy

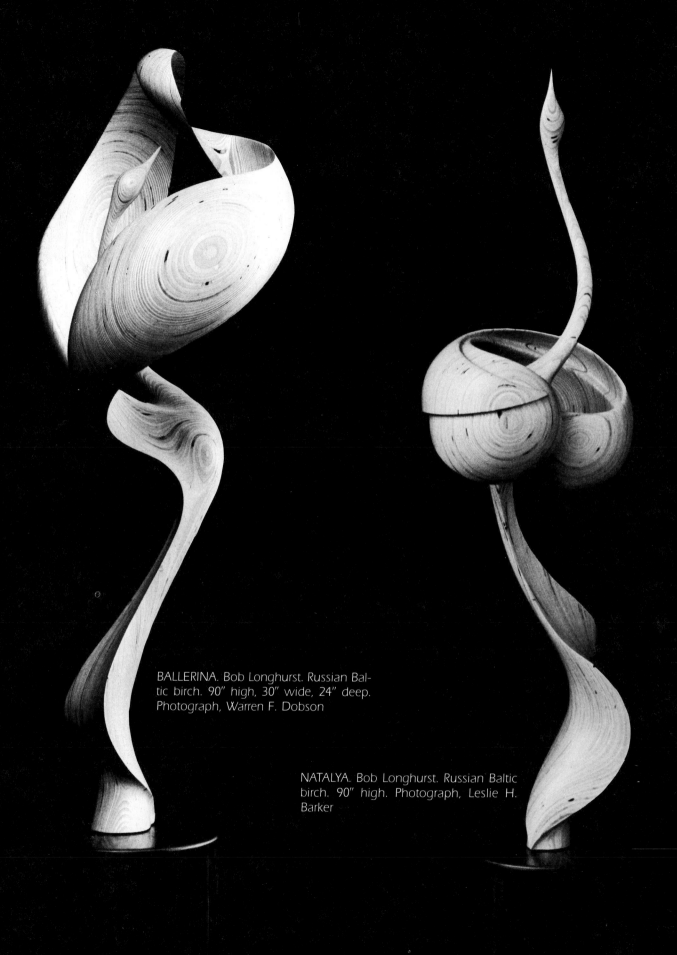

BALLERINA. Bob Longhurst. Russian Baltic birch. 90" high, 30" wide, 24" deep. Photograph, Warren F. Dobson

NATALYA. Bob Longhurst. Russian Baltic birch. 90" high. Photograph, Leslie H. Barker

IRINA. Bob Longhurst. Russian Baltic birch. 7'6" high, 8' wide, 2' deep. Photograph, Edward Miller

OPPOSITE: THE INTERLOCKING WOMAN. A POLYGLYPH. Igor Givotovsky. 1976–1979. Edition of three. Walnut and Brazilian mahogany. 4' high. Collections, Dr. Barry Musikant, New York, NY; Dr. Dixie G. Hamilton, Houston, TX; Wendy Hadley, West Tisbury, MA. Photographs, artist

THE FIRE EATER. Igor Givotovsky. 1976. Walnut, padouk, poplar heartwood, African mahogany, satinwood. 32" high, 19" wide, 11" deep. Photograph, Ed Braverman

THE UNICORN. Igor Givotovsky. 1979. Mixed exotic woods. 16" high, 26" wide, 6" deep. Photograph, Ed Braverman

8

Abstract Sculpture

I often consider abstract art as being to sculpture what the novel is to literature: imaginative, fantasy and fiction. Literal forms of art with readily recognizable subject matter are like nonfiction. All forms communicate specific moods and trains of thought. All must have the formal elements and principles.

In abstraction, color, shape, form, texture, harmony and unity are all present, but they have a visual appeal that is released by the artist's ability to exercise his imagination as he creates. Forms need not be recognizable. There are no bounds for ideas and imagery. Abstract art, also termed nonobjective or nonrepresentational art, can be so enigmatic that a viewer may require an explanation from the artist for its meaning. Though the interpretation may be oblique, the piece should stand as a successful form by the integrated use of the artistic elements and principles.

Abstract art can be as timeless and fresh as the masterpieces of literal art. I have seen many sculptures dated 1980 that could be interchanged easily with ones dated 1960; visual vibrations would be so similar that no update of ideas was apparent. Generally, the pieces selected for this book illustrate a departure, a jumping-off point from an artist's earlier work. Yet some of the earlier work, perhaps not so quickly accepted or exhibited for one reason or another, qualifies for the premise of The New Wave.

Among the photographs submitted, work was generally rejected if there were no signs of change from earlier pieces by the same or other artists. Pieces that were extensively viewed in other publications during the past few years were also rejected. (This acknowledges the importance of an up-to-date photograph file if an artist desires publicity and exposure.)

There are inspirational ideas that can suggest various approaches for your own work such as combining the use of other media including plastic, metal and glass. There are innovative and beautiful surface treatments such as the pierced sculptures by Doug Ayers, made possible by the use of the die grinder. There are

OPPOSITE: *SPIRAL PILLAR* (detail). Jon Brooks. 1978. Oak, ash, beech, birch, maple. One of a series. Each pillar is 12 feet high. Chain-saw carved, hand-gouge textured. Photograph, Oscar Bailey

HANGING/STANDING FORM #3-1-77. Doug Ayers. Padouk. 33" high, 35" wide, 1½" thick. 42" high with base. A negative space exists between the two horizontal thrusts. The bottom portion is supported by the base, the top portion is hung from above. Courtesy, artist

the literal forms made by Doug Hendrickson but transposed into abstraction via the vacuum-form process. Fragmentation has been explored by Jerry Deasy.

I hope that the compilation will be a never-ending source for reference, for appreciation and to serve whatever your individual needs may be at different times. If you lean toward the conservative, literal school of sculpture, perhaps it will entice you to dip your toes in the water's edge, then wade in farther. If you are already exploring new ideas, it may help you take the plunge deeper and deeper. There are uncharted waters in the world of ideas yet to be discovered.

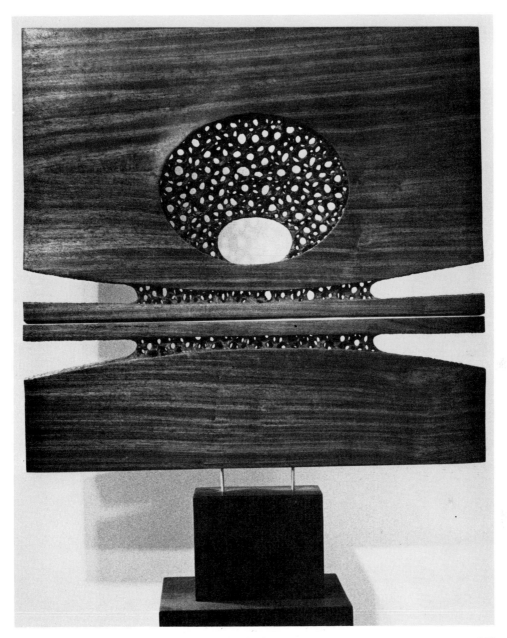

STANDING FORM #8-4-79. Doug Ayers. Black walnut. 33"
high, 25" wide, 2" deep. With black acrylite base, 78" high.
Photograph, Bill J. Wagner

"I am trying to create works that are successful combinations of my psyche and mother nature. All pieces of wood
have pleasing aspects to them and some have 'flaws' that
must be either eliminated or incorporated into the sculptural
form. Using basic design rules, a lot of trial and error, and
bubblings from my inner self, I create works which I liken to a
conversation between myself and the wood. All conversa-
tions are different since no two pieces of wood are the same
and neither am I from one moment to the next. Through
experimentation and insight my vocabulary continues to in-
crease so that I can respond to each piece of wood in more
ways."

Doug Ayers

DOUBLE OUGHT. Doug Hendrickson. 1980. Basswood. 6"
high, 7" wide, 7" deep. Courtesy, Morgan Gallery, Kansas
City, MO

NIKON FM. Doug Hendrickson. 1980. Mahogany. 4" high,
11" wide, 11" deep. Courtesy, Morgan Gallery, Kansas City,
MO

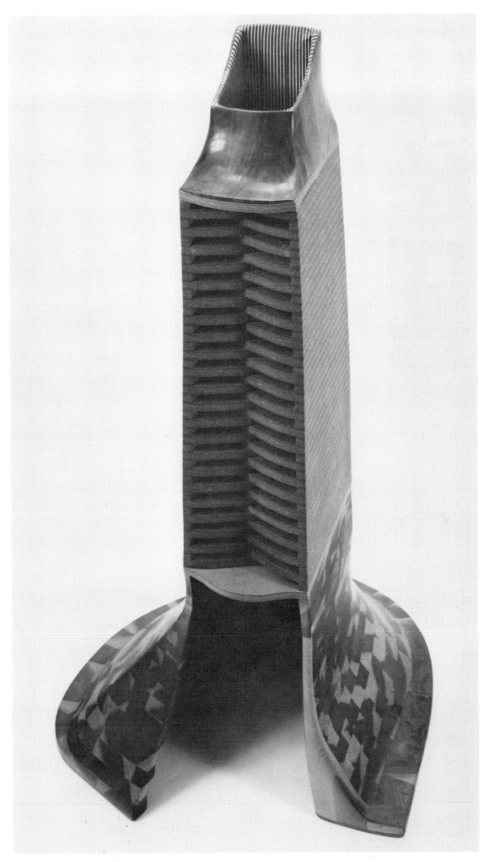

NORTH COAST. William Jaquith Evans. 1980. Laminated redwood base, particle board center section, walnut top. 72" high, 39" wide, 36" deep. Photograph, Richard Sargent

PLASTIC FORM I. Carl E. Johnson. 1979. Walnut. 24" high, 12" wide, 10" deep.

FLUID 5 AND TABLE. Carl E. Johnson. 1980. Walnut. 30" high, 24" wide, 33" deep.

DAMNED JOGGER. Carl E. Johnson. 1977. Walnut. 12" high. Courtesy, artist

UNTITLED. Daniel Yaruss. 1980. Mahogany. 17¼" high, 11" wide, 8" deep. The sculpture was developed from a clay maquette, then a plastic foam model, then the final laminated wood form. Photograph, Dona Meilach

THE PRICE OF ONE ADMISSION IS YOUR MIND. Giles Gilson. 1980. Spalted elm, acrylic, aluminum. 16" high, 8" wide, 7" deep. Photograph, Rick Siciliano

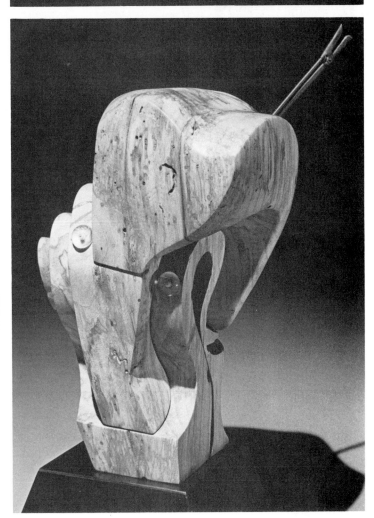

PERCHED FORM. Jerry Deasy. 1980. Oiled koa wood on black base. 3' high. Illustrates the artist's technique of "fragmentation": Laminated wood patterns are cut on a band saw, then reassembled and glued together. In the completed piece, all of the original block is used. Photograph, Tim Osner

BOUND UPWARD. Jerry Deasy. 1980. Zebrawood on black base. 28" high. Photograph, Tim Osner

UNTITLED: Ben Goo. Olive wood with copper. Approximately 50" high. Courtesy, artist

UNTITLED. Ben Goo. Walnut. 96" long. Collection, Roswell Museum and Art Center, Roswell, NM

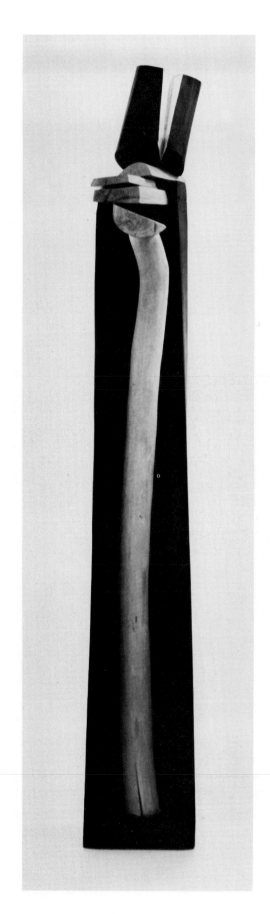

SEARS COURT SCULPTURE. Federico Armijo. 1974. Philippine mahogany. 25' high, 5' wide, 4' deep. Courtesy, artist

HUMAN FORM. Margot DeWit. Mixed woods. 5½' high, 6" wide, 7" deep. Courtesy, A. J. Wood Galleries, Philadelphia, PA

202

ANTECHAMBER OR TORN FREE'S BOX OF CHAOS. Hills Snyder. 1977. Plywood and gray lumber from abandoned buildings. Some polychromed areas. 64" high, 45" wide. The chamber is a metaphor for the body—a passageway to something else. Prototype for an ongoing project of twelve antechambers. Photograph, William Overbeek

PHUMBS. Manuel A. Gomez. 1976. Mahogany, maple, exotic hardwoods. 53½" high, 15" wide, 17" deep. Courtesy, artist

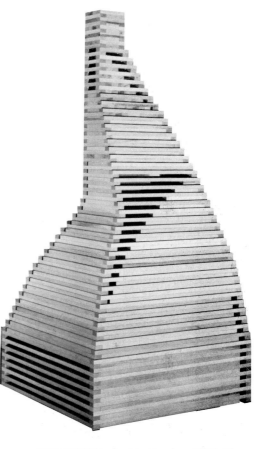

A205 WAVE HILL PROJECT. Jackie Ferrara. 1980. Douglas fir. 9'4" high, 20'2"
wide, 12'5" deep. Courtesy, Max Protetch Gallery, New York. Photograph,
Marbeth

A207 RECALL. Jackie Ferrara. 1980. Pine.
76" high, 37" wide, 37" deep. Courtesy,
Max Protetch Gallery, New York. Photograph, Roy M. Elkind

HOLDING. Leonard C. Cave. 1978.
Wood and bolts. 5' high, 4' wide, 4'
deep. Courtesy, artist

OPPOSITE: UNTITLED. Richard Feese.
1979. Redwood and nails. 75" high, 61"
wide, 27" deep. Courtesy, artist

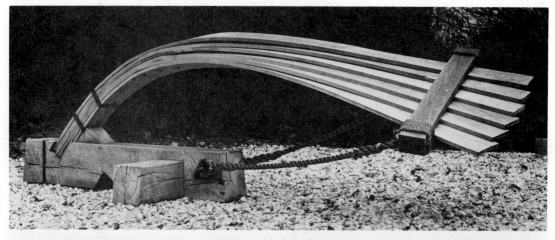

TIDAL. Irving Sabo. 1976. Oak. 29" high, 10" wide, 10'4" long. Courtesy, artist

TOP: TRIBAL. Irving Sabo. 1976. Oak. 26" high, 11'8" long, 32" wide. All pieces, in the form of beams and planking, explore the rigidity of the beams combined with the flexibility of the planking, as in boat hulls. Courtesy, artist

SNAIL. Jesse Roy Fink. 1979. Pine. 4' high, 6' wide, 4' deep. Courtesy, artist

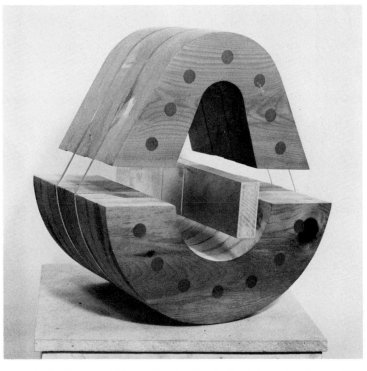

UNTITLED. Ed Vega. 1979. Wood, Plexiglas, aluminum. 22" high, 30" wide, 20" deep. Courtesy, artist

ABOVE, RIGHT: REFRACTED TONDO. Ed Vega. 1979. Pine, walnut, redwood, particle board, Plexiglas and aluminum. 18" high, 16" wide, 9" deep. Courtesy, artist

RIGHT: UNTITLED. Charles M. Kaplan. 1979. Laminated walnut, cherry. 26" high, 15" wide. Courtesy, artist

BELOW: UNTITLED. Daniel Yaruss. Mahogany and Plexiglas. 20" high, 19" wide, 19" deep. Photograph, Dona Meilach

207

CUPULA VOLANTE. Don Schule. 1978. Wood, ceramics, rice paper and bark. 16″ high, 9½″ wide, 10″ deep. Courtesy, artist

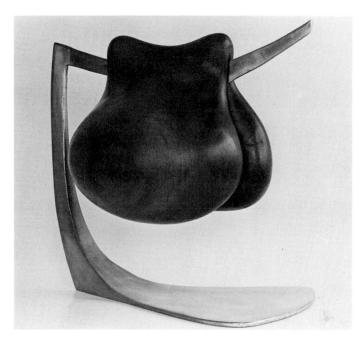

SOFT FORM DIVIDING. Morse Clary. 1979. Black walnut and welded steel. 16" high, 15" wide, 12" deep. Photograph, Cathy Clary

PAIGE'S DRAGON. R. Clark Magruder. Teakwood and metal. 21" high, 36" long, 11" deep. Courtesy, artist

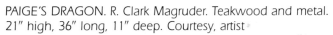

ABOVE, LEFT: TOWERING EGG PYLON. David L. Green. Walnut, leather, horsehair, chicken eggs. 48" high, 18" wide, 18" deep. Photograph, David Watanabe

ABOVE, RIGHT: ELEVATED EGG SHRINE. David L. Green. Horsehair, goose egg, leather, walnut, padouk, acrylic, bronze fittings. 22" high, 15" wide, 15" deep. Photograph, Marie Hanak

OPPOSITE: SUPPORT STRUCTURES. John Kowalewski. 1979. Wood, mixed media. 12' high, 7' wide, 4' deep. Courtesy, artist

LEFT: REVOLVING EGG WIMBLE. David L. Green. Walnut, chamois leather, brass, nylon rod, goose egg. Photograph, Marie Hanak

ROUND WALL. Jane Teller. Walnut. 19"
high, 22" wide, 20" deep. Photograph,
Werner Goodwin

MOON STONES. Irene Gennaro
Cataldo. 1980. Oak with earth pig-
ments. 7" high, 29" wide, 24" deep. Photograph, Roy M. Elkind

WOODPILES. Mark Lindquist. Sculpture created at the Mac-
Dowell Colony, Spring 1979. Courtesy, artist

PART IV
THE ARTISTS and THEIR WORKSPACES

9
Out of Anonymity

What magical processes occur that enable someone to take a fresh log, a dried board, a scrap of lumber, and change it into a finished chair, a precious box, an expressive sculpture? Essentially, it requires a person with artistic vision, motivation, ideas and technical know-how. Additionally there are myriad thought processes, problems to be solved, materials and tools to be selected.

Fortunately, most artistic people do not think about all the aspects of creativity before they start. They create because they must. They meet the hurdles and overcome them one at a time. They try. They make mistakes. They learn. They produce. They deal with the endless details of their craft and spend hours of painstaking labor at saws, workbenches, routers and sanders.

The vision of the artist with finished work piled high about him is often too real. Each hopes to "be discovered"; to have his name become a household word, or, at best, to be able to sell what he makes. He has little time, energy or inclination to battle the windmills of marketing. But today's woodworker is realistic. He learns that merchandising, working fairs, dealing with galleries, clients and publicity are essential. He grudgingly acknowledges that artists can no longer remain anonymous and become known only through their work. Collectors collect artists as well as art.

With this in mind, I have prevailed upon many of the people I interviewed to peer out of their woodshops and let people know who they are, where they work, why they do what they do. I chose to catch them in action rather than posed tintype-like beside a sculpture or piece of furniture. I wanted the sense of working, of taking the reader with me during the interview. My aim was to illustrate the artist's environment; to know how varied the work setups are; how workbenches are arranged; and the spaces that serve as "studios."

Among the more than ninety studios I visited in cities throughout the country, I was intrigued by the range of inventiveness to make an operation more efficient. Where possible, I have shown improvised tools and altered equipment. The reader may find that a photo of a workbench, altered sanding machine or other idea will spark directions for working in his own space with his own tools. I have also visited many commercial woodworking shops to illustrate how industrial operations can become resources for ideas.

BOOTH DISPLAY. Michael Goldfinger and John Wall. Union Woodworks. Used at Rhinebeck, New York, and other fairs, 1980. A modular unit of knock-down plywood panels and a pine frame. The unit is strong and easily varied for change of appearance and configuration at different presentations. It folds into a small space, so it can be easily put into a van. It can be painted different colors; objects may be hung from walls and displayed on stands and tables. Courtesy, Union Woodworks

I spoke with art-fair organizers, gallery owners, museum curators and magazine editors. I would like to share some of the pertinent information about ingredients for success—if selling what one makes is a measure of success. Often "selling" boils down to the right approach to marketing. I am particularly indebted to Ron Isaacson and Deborah Farber-Isaacson of The Mindscape Gallery, Evanston, Illinois, for access to publications they provide for people they represent. Following is a summary of some of the important points.

Tools and techniques used in production shops should be investigated for the limited production woodworker. Often simplified versions of commercial machinery can be created. Several adaptations are illustrated in the following pages. Commercial establishments also rent time on machinery or accept piecework.

Multiple-spindle carving machines are designed to repeat a design one to sixty times simultaneously, depending upon the unit capacity. The machine illustrated will produce sixteen bas-relief panels at one time from one master panel. Some machines will accommodate multiple lathe-carved shapes as well as bas-reliefs. Photographed at Spector Design, Inc., Solana Beach, CA, by Dona Meilach

PUBLICITY

PRESS KITS. These are important for publicity in an upcoming show whether it is to be a one-person or a group event. Press information must be distributed to trade publications and local newspapers well in advance of an actual opening. Often a knowledgeable person is invited to preview a show. Catalogs and mailings also require preliminary information. Good photographs and supplementary information, well written, will help to put you and your work in the news. Often it is not the most newsworthy item that makes a press notice, it is the pre-packaged and well-prepared material—anything that makes it easier for the reporter, the graphic artist and those involved with publishing.

PHOTOGRAPHS. The Isaacsons are emphatic: "There is one requirement that makes or breaks a presentation: PHOTOS. It is nearly impossible to capture the attention of any editor or client without good quality photos: black-and-white glossies for publications, color for selling. Good quality has one meaning: simple, uncluttered well-lighted photos which clearly show the art, preferably one piece per frame. Artist-at-work photos are helpful, but only if they're interesting."

NOTEBOOKS-PORTFOLIOS. A compilation of work and other "sell" items is an invaluable presentation for gallery and art-fair presentations. The portfolio should be neat, attractive, thoughtfully compiled and with good quality photographs in color and/or black and white. It can also include printed announcements of previous shows in which your work was exhibited.

216

Sandblasted wood has infinite textural potential and can be utilized by nonproduction as well as production woodworkers. The principle is to block off some portions of the wood, then sandblast the uncovered portion to achieve desired depths and textures. Soft woods, such as pine and redwood, can have exquisite results so that an ordinary surface becomes extraordinary.

A design carved with laser beams, from Lasercraft, Santa Rosa, CA. Photograph, Dona Meilach

A panel, designed by Suzi Spector for Spector Design, Inc., Solana Beach, California, illustrates a bas-relief made with a multiple-spindle carving machine. The various textures were achieved during the initial carving, then different abrasive grades of a whip sander were used for the background followed by a final hand sanding. Photographs, Dona Meilach

Positive reviews of your work from newspapers, magazines and other activities all help. (They were probably achieved with a good press kit.) A résumé and list of people who have already collected or commissioned your work are advisable, if the list is impressive.

DISPLAY AND VISUAL MERCHANDISING

In today's competitive market, the professional designer-craftsman has to realize that the creation of quality work alone is not enough to ensure sales. The manner in which the work is presented has much bearing on potential sales and repeat business. The requirements fall under the term VISUAL MERCHANDISING, which the Isaacsons interpret with this premise: "If a good product is effectively presented to the right audience, sales must follow."

For displays the following factors are required:

A COMPLIMENTARY ENVIRONMENT. This refers to display pedestals and background. Emphasis is placed on using materials that compliment your work.

FLEXIBILITY. Make displays and units that can be easily moved, changed in shape and size for any given area.

ROOM FOR PEOPLE TO WALK AROUND, STEP BACK, OBSERVE. Avoid straight aisles. A zigzag path forces people to slow down, stop and look.

More points deal with filling in stock, keeping hourly inventories if you are manning your own booth, wrapping merchandise so that unwrapped pieces will shout "thief!"

Help your customer visualize an object in the customer's own environment. Provide plants, swatches of fabrics and wallpapers and squares of wood-grained flooring to simulate colors of furniture, floors and walls. Have measurements handy for every piece. Use business cards with large type so even older customers will not have to squint to read your name and number.

If you are present when pieces are being sold, try to work at some aspect of your craft: carving, sanding, sketching. This encourages people to talk to you, ask questions, approach you. It lets the people handle the merchandise, and gives you the opportunity to talk about your work and to use selling tactics.

With the increased recognition of, and respect for, multiple-production and limited-edition pieces, more information has become available regarding the business of art. Watch your specialized woodworking magazines and general craft and art publications for seminars and conferences offering insights into the varied aspects of financial success at the business of art. These two terms have not been wedded successfully in the past, but the courtship is becoming warmer.

Fads in arts and crafts swell and ebb, but the need for woodwork is constant and can always escalate in the right climate. As merchandisers and the buying public recognize that the individual craftsperson can compete in a production society, the opportunities are burgeoning for an artist with wood to realize a comfortable living doing what he loves most to do.

Federico Armijo built a showroom-gallery in Albuquerque, New Mexico. He presents not only his designs in wood, metal and stone, but the work of other artists as well. The gallery, which is in the "Old Town" historic zone, is curvilinear and contemporary. Exterior materials and design blend beautifully with the adobe American Indian style of the area. Federico's actual workshop is in an old factory building shared with other craftsmen in another part of the city. Photograph, Dona Meilach

219

STANDING FORM 2-5-79. Doug Ayers. Black walnut on a black acrylite base. Sculpture only: 21" high, 22½" wide, 3" deep. Photograph, David J. Russell

To achieve the lacy negative offset areas in his sculptures (see also pages 194, 195). Doug Ayers glues boards together for the necessary width, then curves the surfaces of both sides of the circle with a power plane. After creating the design, he "honeycombs" the wood with a die grinder fitted with a wood-carving burr. In this photograph he is carving through the routed areas to achieve the lacework pattern. He finishes and sands all other areas, then blows the dust out of the holes. For contrast, lacework areas are dyed with leather dyes. The entire piece is then given a final finish with Danish natural oils. The sculpture will be hung by a thin wire from the ceiling so it can turn freely in the air currents.

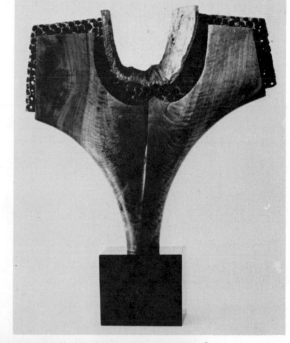

BELOW: A variety of tools Doug uses for his work: TOP LEFT: An electric drill with flexible shaft, foam rubber pad and sanding disk. CENTER TOOLS: Six die grinders of different models and brands. RIGHT: A power plane. Photographs, Dona Meilach

Jon Brooks in his studio, surrounded by his handmade furniture. His studio and home reflect the same kind of conceptualization and design as his furniture; all are created from tree sections that he finds in the nearby New Hampshire countryside.

DEMERITT CHAIR. Jon Brooks. Elm wood. 50" high, 27" wide, 34" deep. Photographs, Mark Lindquist

Jeffrey A. Briggs emphasizes the importance of the drawing before creating any dimensional sculptural forms. Trained as a painter, Jeffrey feels that the completed watercolor painting is, in a sense, the final work. "Everything I do after that is perfecting the piece technically ... making it three-dimensional."

To create a wall clock, wall mirror, or any of the myriad other designs for which he has become well known, Jeffrey first makes several quick design sketches. He uses a heavy graphite stick, which enables him to achieve the flowing forms. A tracing of the final design is rendered in watercolors. The color shadings help Jeff to perceive the carving in three dimensions. In all his pieces, he combines natural light-colored woods with darker woods for the swirling hair that has become his trademark.

For three-dimensional free-standing pieces, as opposed to wall relief sculptures, the working sketch will be a clay or wax model rather than a watercolor.

When carving torsos, Jeffrey works from positive to negative areas and avoids undercutting until final decisions are made. Working tools are a band saw for the initial shaping, then a die grinder, chisels and carving knives.

In all the processes, hundreds of decisions must be made regarding scale, color, woods to use, grain directions, where to laminate what pieces and which elements will be at which levels. Most pieces are accomplished with one to three laminate layers.

After all sanding and varnishing are accomplished, the clock movements or mirror is set into the sculpture. For finished examples see pages 27, 29 and 32. Photographs, Tom Wilson

The second-story loft work area of a two-story factory building in a San Francisco industrial area houses the Satisfaction-Promise Woodworking Company, owned by Saumitra Lewis Buchner. The company creates an interesting mix of custom furniture and cabinetry for corporate offices, and at the same time produces cabinets for electronic medical components and minicomputers.

Buchner explains: "Satisfaction-Promise exists for a broader reason than to just succeed financially. The business creates a link between the outer world of craftsmanship, design and contracting and the inner world of meditation. For us, the real fulfillment of a project lies not only in its final appearance but rather in the consciousness in which the project is carried out and completed. Work done in a good consciousness is a form of meditation and if, as a small group of craftspeople, we can do our daily work with a real feeling of inner peace and joy, then every day we can feel we have made a little progress toward realizing our own inner potential.

"Most of the workers of Satisfaction-Promise are students of a meditation teacher or spiritual master named Sri Chinmoy, a highly respected authority on Bhakti Yoga.

"The name was given to the group by Sri Chinmoy, and the name reflects the business's commitment to its customers and to an inner promise to one's inmost self to achieve something which will give a real and lasting satisfaction." Photograph, Dona Meilach

The conference table pictured on page 66, under construction, shows the boat-hull concept. Courtesy, Saumitra Lewis Buchner

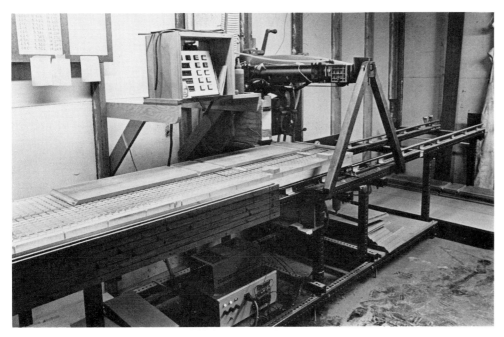

A customized and improvised computer-controlled V-grooving saw was designed by Saumitra Buchner and a few friends, including an electronics engineer, a machinist and his shop foreman.

The saw part is built from an old DeWalt 14-inch radial arm saw. The 8-foot Plexiglas bed has a grid routed into it, and by inserting a rubber gasket the operator can define an area under the work piece which is connected to a vacuum pump. The vacuum pressure holds the work to the bed with tremendous force. The bed advances along steel rails driven by a computer "stepping motor." The stepping motor is fed pulses from the control circuitry, and the distance between each cut is set with thumb-wheel switches on the control panel. This allows accuracy of ±.005" between each cut. The blade cuts partway through the bottom veneer, and tape applied to that surface acts as a hinge when the V-shaped groove is folded up into a mitered corner. The machine has been running for three years with almost no repairs.

RIGHT: Finished cabinets.

BELOW: Detail of groove is shown at center, and at left is a folded, mitered corner. Photographs, Dona Meilach

Leonard C. Cave develops huge log sculptures with a chain saw to shape out mass areas, then follows with chisels of various sizes for detailing. Leonard deals with the concepts of large masses and their relationship to space within and around to achieve a compositional balance in both his sculpture and furniture. Courtesy, artist

Morse Clary refines a shape. Courtesy, artist

Bill Chappelow's workshop-studio is in an old house in the mountains of Southern California. He is restoring and refurbishing it in whatever extra time he finds. Outside, logs are piled high, aged and dried. He also purchases or trades his logs for about two-thirds of his needs. These are the exotic woods he uses to create toys, utensils, scales and other objects in a growing line that sells readily through galleries and fairs.

Bill uses old and new tools, improvised clamps and other "Rube Goldberg-like" aids. A butcher's meat-cutting saw, bought as an outdated tool, is invaluable for cutting large logs. He still uses two antique turning tools he purchased at a flea market. Photographs, Dona Meilach

David Carlin demonstrates his carving technique in ivory and wood during a woodworkers' seminar. David says: "The Japanese netsuke miniature carvings are the only company from which I can draw inspiration. Not being bound by traditional subjects (as were the Japanese) I can experience creative freedoms of the artist in this format. So much peace is needed to keep the ideas flowing, and the price of peace keeps getting higher."

About his tools, David adds: "I use simple hand tools and much sanding, scraping and polishing. It's the touch of a lifetime of practice and lots of enthusiasm."

And about design: "I move the materials: wood ivory, porcelain, to suit the demands of form and balance. Surface quality and carefully designed textures dictate the tones and colors of the forms. The subjects I use need these qualities that appear to enlarge their size and meaning although the actual piece may be only 3 to 6 mm. long. Photograph, Dona Meilach

OPPOSITE: Charles B. Cobb stands in the doorway of the studio-workshop he built on the back of his property twenty-three yards behind his home in Santa Rosa, California. The shop is exterior plywood and drywall with natural lighting via a roof that is half steel and half white Plexiglas. Very large doors on the shop allow for easy movement of objects in and out. Recycled redwood was used for the siding and some of the worktables.

The large interior space allows him to have several projects in work simultaneously. He says, "I think of myself as a sculptor; I have worked in several media: plastic, clay, metal, but wood is the best. I like the feel, the smell, everything about it as a medium for creativity. I strive for a fluidity of form and I am more interested in design than technique. I use basic, simple methods of joinery, learning new ones as I need them to express the design concept. Working wood is a constant learning experience."

Charles explained that at first he made traditional objects just to make money. Then he became braver and worked in more contemporary forms, creating bigger and more expensive objects. "When my prices jumped from something that cost sixty dollars to a piece of furniture that cost six hundred dollars and someone stood in the street and said, 'I'll take it,' it was mind boggling—but comforting." Photographs, Dona Meilach

228

Michael Coffey's studio in Poultney, Vermont, is an improvisationist's delight. For his wide range of laminated furniture pieces he has had to find solutions for myriad creative problems. He devised unorthodox tools and techniques for carving masses of wood fast and accurately. Over the years, he has developed increased skill with the chain saw to do rough and finished carving with extreme accuracy and speed, and with more versatility than the traditional sculptor's gouge could accomplish. He also uses disc sanders, air and electric grinders, and other tools associated with metal, automobile body work, and other industrial procedures.

In addition to a space for his own work, Coffey's studio serves as a two-year full-time professional woodworking school for six students at a time.

BELOW: Coffey relaxes in his large rocking lounge chair titled APHRODITE, made of Mozambique. It is 54" high, 90" wide and 28" deep. Photographs, Rich Baldinger

This unusual handmade door leads to the idyllic studio of Frank E. Cummings. The intricate hand-carved gears in the door lock are visible through the clear glass panel mounted between the series of wood panels culled from shipping pallets. The door leads from a study to the studio, which has been built above the garage of his two-story house. In his studio at home, Frank likes to be surrounded by materials from nature that help provide his inspiration. He gathered some of them during a year of living and studying with craftsmen in Ghana, West Africa. He often uses silver, gold, bone and ivory with traditional jewelry techniques in various detailing in his clocks, mirrors and furniture.

Much of Frank's wood supply is garnered "by keeping my ears and eyes open. Whenever I hear a chain saw in the neighborhood, I head for the sound and am usually able to bring home portions of tree trunks that might otherwise be discarded in the city dump." Photographs, Dona Meilach

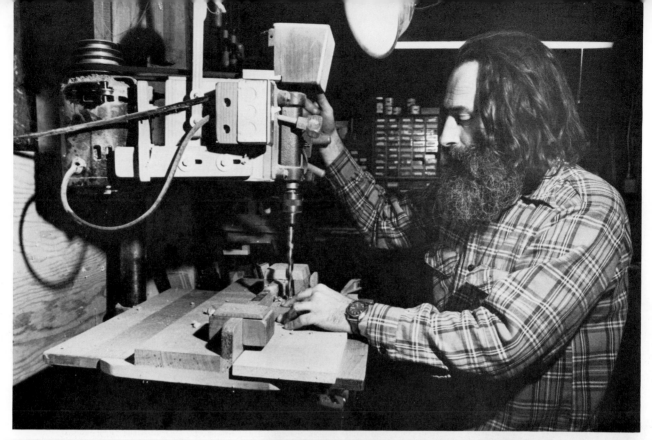

Jack Dohany works at his "home-brew" drill press to make parts for a distinctive line of toys sold through galleries and exclusive toy shops and directly at art fairs. His toys have become collectors' items (see page 46). He works at home in his basement and garage with a variety of inventive tools. These tools, though marvelously monsterish looking, have a unique mechanistic-sculptural quality about them. Parts are often taken from other contexts, such as (ABOVE and BELOW) the boat-steering handle that propels his drill press. "I like the feel of the wooden handle."

Jack prefers to sell his toys directly to customers at Renaissance fairs and other art fairs along the West Coast. He says it's "horrible to make something beautiful and then just put it in a box and ship it off. I enjoy seeing the customer appreciate the object, play with it, handle it, and I like to imagine a toy in the hands of a particular child."

Jack Dohany's "home-brew" drill press. The motor and arbor are a unit, moving together. Their weight is counterbalanced by a stacked unit of coffee cans filled with cement (50 pounds), not visible (behind the drill press). There are an upper and a lower depth stop and 11 inches of vertical travel. He also has a commercially made drill press, "but the home-brew is much pleasanter to use." Jack made the "boat-steering wheel" that is used to raise and lower the unit. "It looks nice and feels beautiful."

The drawer immediately beneath the drill press is customized to hold the drill bits. It slides out easily on ball-bearing drawer glides.

LEFT: A pneumatic sander is mounted on an A-frame that can easily fold up for storage and be put out of the way.

Note that each piece of equipment is fitted with an old Electrolux vacuum cleaner which collects the sawdust. He prefers these to a central exhaust system. They are quite inexpensive, and readily available at flea markets, and reliable. Each is wired to turn on with the tool. They are mounted at the front of the tool so they are easily accessible for cleaning. They eliminate any possibility of sawdust's being exhausted into the outdoor environment.

RIGHT: A homemade 4" × 36" belt sander that was made very simply has provided years of trouble-free use. Jack's premise is that "often, when commercially made equipment fails, it's difficult to find parts. When you create your own machinery, you know every part that goes into it and can quickly replace anything that wears out or malfunctions."

A toy involving a clown tumbling down a ladder requires multiple routed holes in uprights to receive rungs. An estimate from a commercial tool maker to develop a suitable multiple-spindle router was $40,000. It took a year of planning and perfecting, but Jack invented and created the tool to do the same job at a cost of $400. The resulting eight-spindle router (open view) is built in an A-frame format. The table rides on the front of the A-frame on adjustable rosewood bearings (not visible) and is moved upward by pressing a foot pedal. The ladder side rests in a holder which can be moved horizontally by operating a lever with the left hand. The holder is a vise. A one-horsepower motor resides on the back of the A-frame. Steel cables go from the pedal up to the pulleys and back down to the table.

BELOW: After the holes are drilled for the ladder rungs, all the parts are assembled in a specially designed "ladder assembly vise." The assembly is so strong and reliable that no glues are used. Toys are guaranteed, so if any are broken or pulled apart repair is easily made. This device holds the two ladder sides and eight ladder rungs in proper relation to one another. Cranking the handle causes the ladder sides to be pressed securely onto the rungs, or vice versa. The result is a completed ladder in ten seconds. The ladder, of darker wood than the vise, can be seen in the vise.

Jack holds a ladder to show what the machine accomplishes. The cover, which is closed when the machine is in use, keeps the unit clean.

234

"This strange contraption," says Jack, "is a sanding lathe built as an experiment, but it worked so well that a 'final version' was never built." Basically, there is a rotating shaft faced by gimbal-mounted (sort of) belt sanders, one with a coarse belt and one with a fine belt. The rotating shaft can be adjusted horizontally and can be replaced with other shafts. Various objects can be attached to the shaft (and thus be made to rotate) in various ways. The shaft's rotational direction is governed, through relays, by the belt-sander switches so that whichever belt sander is in operation, the shaft rotates in the proper direction.

Detail of central portion of sanding lathe showing a toy part, the unicycle clown handle grip. The grip is cut from a ¾-inch dowel; then both ends of the grip are sanded round and smooth in about fifteen seconds. The grip is held gently but firmly in a rubber-banded holder. First it is shaped round with a coarse belt sander, then smoothed with the fine belt sander. All photographs, Dona Meilach

Jerry Deasy's photograph, sent to me "for laughs" and titled "artist going mad," points up some of the noncreative aspects of being an artist . . . the importance of photography and attention to even the smallest details—specks of dust. Courtesy, artist

Margot DeWit's large-scale pieces require ample studio space with high ceilings and enough stools and ladders to enable her to reach the lofty heights of her sculptures. This piece, CONSTRUCTION VII, is made of wood, resin and bamboo. 7½' high, 1½' wide, 2' deep. Courtesy, A. J. Wood Galleries, Philadelphia, PA

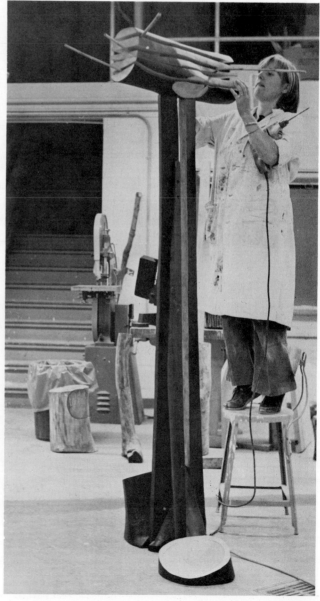

Bruce Decker works at a vise and clamp he devised for holding a walking-stick shaft while he shapes it with a spokeshave. With this wooden tool, he can use the spokeshave in all possible positions and keep his knuckles clear of the bench edge at all times. Fine carving and signing can also be accomplished with the shaft held in position.

Detail showing one-half of the vise in use and (LEFT) unclamped from the bench. This device can be used independently of, or in conjunction with, the vise built into most woodworking benches. Courtesy, artist

237

Winslow Eaves refers to his sculptures as "large tree-carvings," and many appear in public places and private collections in New Hampshire, New York, Florida and elsewhere. In addition to his sculptural commissions, Winslow has a continuing involvement in a New Hampshire program, "Artists in the Schools." Tree sculptures, created with the aid of students, are placed on the grounds of various schools.

ABOVE: Winslow is perched on his SCULPTOPUS in the playground of the Grantham School, Sutton, New Hampshire.

Winslow Eaves, foreground, works with students of the Kearsage Regional High School to develop a tree sculpture titled SEVEN-ELEVEN.

238

E

As part of the Artists in the Schools program, other public agencies are involved. The National Guard, as a training experience, moved the sculpture (OPPOSITE), SCULPTOPUS, from the original work site to the front of the school, where it was finished in place.

Another view of SCULPTOPUS, finished and mounted on concrete blocks. All photographs, Terry Rayno

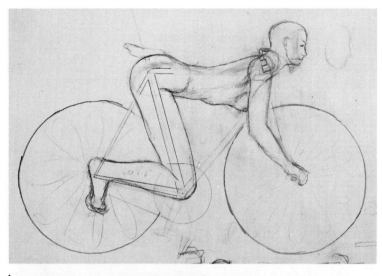

1

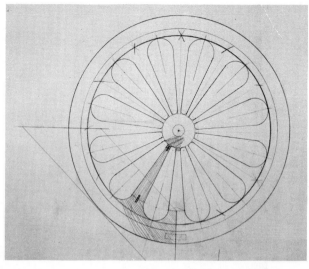

2

3

Doug Freerksen likes the imagery of human and animal forms in new contexts. A sculpture may develop as described in the accompanying photos:

1. Each piece begins with an idea, roughly sketched. For proportion this drawing was made over an actual bicycle.

2. For many practical reasons, a detailed drawing is made of each piece, using necessary drafting tools. By drawing the wheel, for example, Doug knows the amount of lumber needed and how to assemble the piece.

3. Frequently Doug makes a full-size model from corrugated cardboard. This allows him to ascertain the feasibility of a project, to change any proportions or angles, and to solve any unforeseen problems without wasting materials and time.

4. A No. 2 white common pine was used for the wheels. The initial shape was built in the same way one would build a heavy picture frame; then the wheel pattern was drawn directly on the clamped-up wooden square.

4

5

6

7

8

5. A large adjustable boring tool was used in the drill press to achieve a clean, smooth curve where the spokes contact the wheel rim.

6. To prevent the wheel from flying apart as it turned, a slow RPM was required. Doug improvised a lathe with a head speed of no more than 200 RPM and a space for a 27-inch diameter turning. He used a Shimpo potter's wheel (for ceramics) clamped sideways on his heavy workbench, then turned the wheel in the normal manner.

7. When the outer rim of the wheel was finished on the improvised lathe, all excess wood was removed from the inside of the now round "picture frame." Wedge-shaped wood spokes were assembled between the wheel and the hub.

8. The cycle pieces were assembled, using clamps and dowels before gluing. Then all final details were accomplished using hand and power tools.

9. The finished sculpture: DREAM CYCLE. Doug Freerksen. 1980. White pine. 48" high 72" long, 16" wide. All parts move as on a normal bicycle. Photographs, courtesy artist

9

Michael N. Graham's containers have created a great impact on the design of contemporary boxes. His McCallister boxes, which appeared in my earlier book, "Small Wood Objects as Functional Sculpture," have been exhibited around the country and widely emulated. Michael constantly develops unsuspected and surprising new shapes. Where does he get his ideas?

Michael explains: "Ideas appear to be for the asking. It is possible that most new ideas/inventions come from nothing more than problem solving: seeing either that something is wrong and should be changed, or merely wondering if it could be different or better. I think it is this discipline to stop and question that becomes the incubator of new ideas.

"If one were to look at a large number of McCallister box designs, a logical progession of questioning from one design to the next could be seen. Very few of the designs or techniques that I have used have been spontaneous conceptions. I spend a lot of time drawing. Normally there are many areas of a given drawing that strike me as not being right. These areas are eliminated and what is left is carried over and expanded upon in later drawings becoming the basis of each new design."
Photograph, Robert Howell

Bruce Guttin's recent creative forays are in the studies of old shoes and boots despite the rib-cage structure shown here. "Not just any shoe," emphasizes Bruce. "The shoe must have been worn and from a specific time and style period."

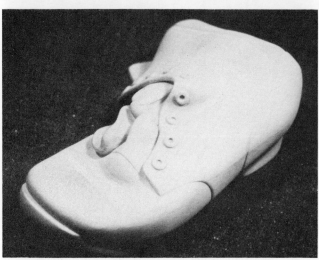

OLD BOOT. Bruce Guttin. 1979. Pine. 9" high, 11½" wide, 3½" deep. Courtesy, artist

Hugh Gundry's display area is a large storefront window in an off-the-main-street area of Pasadena, California, headed by the sign "Whimsical Wood-crafts." His workshop is next to the store, his living quarters, upstairs. The operations he uses for making toys and other objects are carefully "hand automated" so that he can employ helpers for the easier operations. A few of his designs became "accidents" and resulted in imaginative new objects directed to a broader market. For example, a "square wheel" toy is marketed as a back-massage device. It led to other massage devices which are now sold in department stores and boutiques. Hugh also merchandises his handmade toys and other objects through art and craft shows. Says Hugh, "my informal little showroom has grown up into a real hardwood toy-shop."

Hugh works at an improvised sanding machine that he designed. Photographs, Dona Meilach

Manuel A. Gomez, educated as a sculptor, now works with wood as an avocation which he "subsidizes with a full-time job." His graphics and sculpture repeat the forms of his hand-carved combs, and vice versa.

The combs range from about 10½ inches high and 3½ inches wide. Each has a historical imagery and/or an African art inspiration. They are created lovingly from a variety of exotic hardwoods. Photograph, Dona Meilach

Margery Eleme Goldberg is proud of her completely equipped shop in which she has trained a number of other women woodworkers since 1973. Her sculptures and furniture have been exhibited widely and purchased by major collectors. She observes, "The attitudes of males regarding females around traditionally male-dominated equipment isn't always enlightened." She believes that women have a great deal of flexibility and aptitude for working with machinery and wood. They can build and finish as well as make convincing salespeople in a gallery. At right is Margery in her Washington, D.C., shop with two apprentices. Courtesy, artist

Erik Gronborg bisects a log of avocado wood. The small, thoroughly organized two-car garage he has converted into his study is divided: one portion houses his woodworking, the other portion his ceramics. He is nationally known for his work in both media. Courtesy, artist

Ben Goo surveys the wood model for a commissioned sculpture to be poured in bronze in the State of Arizona. The wood, viable as a finished piece, is the pattern and model for the sand-cast bronze. Photograph, Charles R. Conley

Giles Gilson has worked in many media. He applies his knowledge of industrial time/motion study to his studio. By utilizing efficient thinking and the methodology of graphic arts, patternmaking, engineering and so forth he has developed a variety of accessories for standard equipment and devised new equipment for specific purposes. Giles is shown with his turned and carved boxes, sculpture and furniture in his display booth at Rhinebeck, New York. Photograph, Jeff Secendorf

Giles demonstrates his homemade table saw. The fence is held in alignment with the saw blade by a cable beneath the table and it is clamped in place by the lever lock. Observe the hand-carved trunnion lock near the elevation wheel at the front of the saw. Photograph, Betsy Cotton

A drawing-board sander designed and built by Giles Gilson. The machine tilts to a convenient angle so the operator can use it for light spindle sanding. With the table removed, it is used for a foam-back disk- and drum-sanding operation. Photographs, Giles Gilson

BELOW: A router rail designed and built by Giles Gilson is used for planing glued-up panels or for any board assembly that is too large to fit a conventional planer. It can also be used for dadoing panels, slotcutting, etc. It disassembles and hangs on the wall for storage.

Robert and Joanne Herzog's studio is in a garage attached to their house in Sonoma County, California. The forms of their desks and jewelry cabinets have a beautiful fluidity. Joinery and inherent wood patterns are an integral part of the total design. Their work is often distinguishable by a heart-shaped dovetail joint used in large pieces. Readily marketable hand-carved jewelry boxes and smaller objects are efficiently produced for year-round shipping. Photograph, Dona Meilach

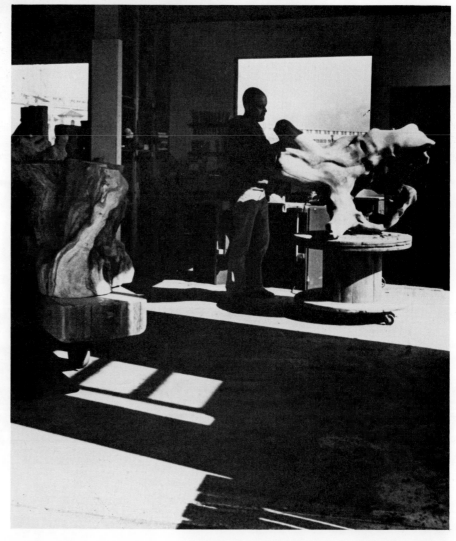

Nicholas Hampson has one of the most unique studio spaces I found. It is in a long warehouse turned into workshop and storage area at one of the San Francisco piers. The enviable views of the bay and the Oakland bridge were magnificent under an incredibly blue sky the day I climbed to the roof to photograph his sculptures. He creates sculptures and seating from huge stumps he finds along the river banks of northern California and Oregon. Photograph, Dona Meilach

Lawrence B. Hunter shapes one of the elements for the intricate, completely hand-carved clocks for which he is well known. Photograph, Kay Colby

Richard Hoptner's studio in a bedroom of his apartment in a Philadelphia suburb is almost hospital clean. He uses no power tools; all pieces are completely hand carved, using a variety of basic "not very exotic instruments—just love and tenderness." Photograph, Dona Meilach

Tyler James Hoare has a neat, organized object-filled studio. It is like a sculptural fantasy environment behind a storefront on a business street of Berkeley, California. Photograph, Dona Meilach

OPPOSITE: Doug Hendrickson has a unique approach to design and to the sculptural forms he develops. He seeks objects from the real world, then thermoforms a sheet of vinyl over them using a vacuum-form process. When the hot sheet of vinyl cools it holds the general form of the object over which it was stretched. A careful study and analysis of the resulting form becomes the basic imagery for the wood carving. On the workbench is a laminated block with a partially carved surface taken from a thermoformed shape.

Doug explains his theory and procedure: "I select objects that seem to very special (archetypical) to a special group. For example, to a photographer the Nikon is THE camera, not a Kodak or a Pentax—but a Nikon. After deciding what object to develop, I thermoform white vinyl plastic over it. This allows me to see the form without complications of color, details and specifics. At this point the object (Nikon) looks as if it has a skin of white plastic stretched over it—in fact, it does. In this pristine white

state I can study it to see if it has the visual qualities I am interested in. No matter how important an idea may be, if it doesn't hold up visually it just doesn't make it for me. If at this point in the process everything works, I carve a replica of the thermoform out of wood. The carving is quite true to the thermoformed object, with just enough variation and change to keep it visually alive. I am looking for a wedding of form and idea.

"Some of my pieces evoke amazing responses from viewers. One in particular is a carving of a Craftsman screwdriver from Sears, Roebuck. Viewers whose 'set' or 'schema' is such that they deal with screwdrivers in real life have looked at this piece and been able to tell me the color, where to buy it and how much it costs. With as little visual information as possible I try to reveal all there is to know about a specific object to persons of particular outlooks. We only see what we know."

All photographs courtesy, artist

ABOVE: The white vinyl thermoformed shape. FRONT: The partially carved form.

Doug Hendrickson's studio with a carving in progress clamped to the workbench.

SCREWDRIVER. LEFT: Thermoformed plastic skin model. RIGHT: Finished carving.

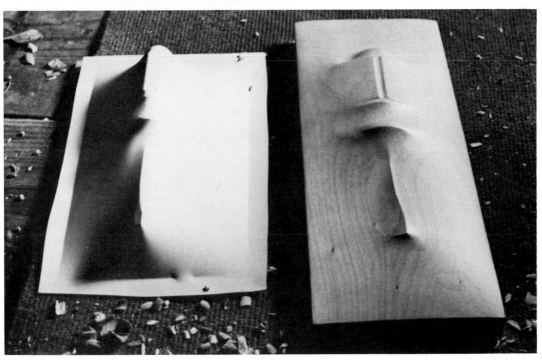

Carl E. Johnson creates doors, sculptures and furniture in his studio, which is a converted garage. He often combines leaded glass with the doors, for which he has won several prizes. He continually explores the possibility of wood-in-motion concepts such as the "drip-form" wood sculptures and "knotted" wood sculpture and furniture (pages 79 and 198). All together, they illustrate Carl's versatility and individual trompe l'oeil statements.

TRI-DOOR II (exterior). Carl E. Johnson, 1980. Mahogany and leaded glass. Door: 80" high, 40" wide. Glass: 78" high, 20" wide.

LA DOOR II. Carl E. Johnson. 1979. Mahogany and leaded glass. Private home, Indio, CA.

Construction details of laminated portions that will become stylized knot shapes. One "knot" will serve as the door pull.

Clamping the finished carved panels to the door.

Interior of TRI-DOOR II (detail). All photographs, Carl E. Johnson

The smooth rounded shapes are in contrast to the chiseled texture of the back surface.

Sara Jaffe sands a wood upright for a bed commissioned by a large hotel. She shares studio space in an artists' building in Berkeley, California. Educated as an architect, Sara became more fascinated by woodworking than by the total building. She apprenticed to a well-known woodworker for basic knowledge and experience.

RIGHT: An arch and bannister of Peruvian walnut in a private residence. Sara Jaffe. Photographs, Dona Meilach

The central working area of Sterling King's studio is flanked by his essential tool rack designed to hold a variety of shaping instruments. "Such industrial equipment, improvised and used by the artist, is most responsible for the flowering and flourishing of the handmade furniture and sculpture in the past few decades," believes Sterling. The portable rack (on wheels) holds a circular sanding machine fitted with inner tubes and foam-rubber backing pads, die grinder, orbital sander, body grinder, planers and essential sound deadeners and respirator.

On Sterling's workbench is a walnut cocktail table, in progress, titled FASCINATION RIDGE #4. His first floor studio beneath his home overlooking the Pacific ocean is open to the air, water, waves and mountains; they serve as his source of inspiration and pleasure. Photographs, Dona Meilach

Jon Kaplan shares a workshop space/studio with Federico Armijo and Steve Madsen in Albuquerque, New Mexico. Jon makes beautiful looms for weaving. Although the looms do not fit the premise of the book the laminating process he devised was so practical, inexpensive and easy to duplicate that I chose to include it here. Jon was delighted to share it.

The laminating press is made from two scrap I-beams, welded together to form a rectangle. Another I-beam is suspended in between these with heavy-duty garage-door springs. Three 12-ton automobile jacks press the beam down on the wood to be laminated. The press part is lined with ⅛-inch polypropylene to prevent the glue from adhering to the metal.

Jon Kaplan also shares his improvised pneumatic drill press design. He says: "If one needs to drill many holes, as we do for a loom, the ideal setup is to drill them all at once. A unit for that purpose costs about four thousand dollars. The next option is to drill one hole at a time—faster. Our air-feed attachment does just that. It also controls the feed rate up and down so the operator can keep both hands on the work."

The two-way, or double-actuating, air cylinder is attached to the main casting of the press. A wire is wrapped around the press handle and then back to the cylinder. The effect is that as the cylinder is actuated, the wire spins the press handle, which raises and lowers the quill. Flow gauges on each end of the cylinder control the rate at which the quill moves. A foot control, used to actuate the system, is fed by a filter, regulator and lubricator. Photographs, Dona Meilach

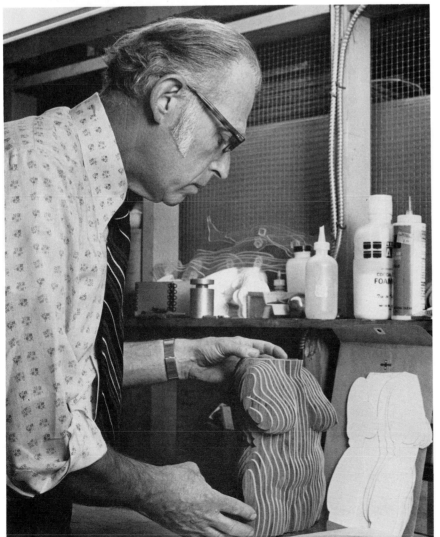

Reuben H. Karrol's sculptures begin with photographs he takes of a female form. He then mentally extracts shapes from the interior to achieve the necessary outer contours. Photographs are reduced to drawings, then a series of patterns are made from these contours. The patterns are used directly to cut the material; the drawings become the guide for positioning the sections while the piece is being assembled in three dimensions. The two dimensional drawing can be seen on the table and the cardboard patterns are at the rear. Photograph, Victor's Photography

257

William H. Livingston, in addition to the pipes and letter openers shown on page 41, enjoys making beautifully turned bowls. He has created a variety of devices and simple-to-use procedures such as this press for gluing faceplate blocks on trays and bowls. He says, "I developed this system because I couldn't find parallel clamps with a deep enough throat to clamp the faceplate blocks onto. The frames are used as extension table supports for my band saw when not being used as a press."

BELOW: A double jackshaft is devised for turning large bowls. "I turn most of my bowls green, some as heavy as 150 pounds. This lathe setup yields low speeds. It is simple and inexpensive and increases the versatility of the machine."

ABOVE: Bowl with faceplate block still attached.

He has also developed a useful approach for making wheels that could be adapted to portions of other types of objects and to objects themselves. The wheels are made from scraps. Pieces are first band-sawed to a rough diameter, and ¼-inch holes are drilled in the center. The shapes are mounted on the chuck between two round blocks with a ball bearing between the block and wheels. The bearing is placed dead center so it pushes against the block but does not touch the shaft. Steel washers are mounted between each tailstock block and between each wheel.

All four wheels are shaped with a home-forged and -ground lathe tool. They are also sanded while still on the lathe. The steel washers, as spacers, make the entire project so simple and fast that the whole process requires about 15 minutes.

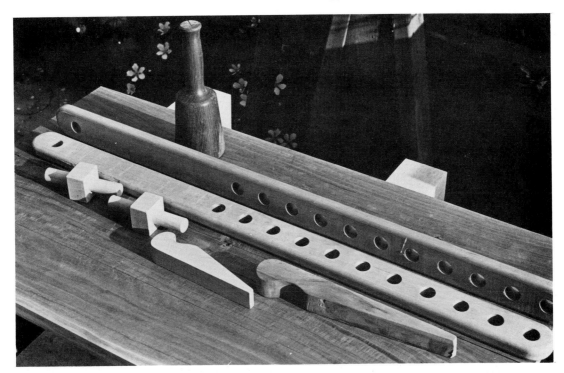

Handmade adjustable wood bar clamps are devised from a very old concept, but William has developed his own variation. The pegs between the bars can be round, but then one has to pound the wedges both in and out. If the pegs are turned, leaving a square between the dowels, these can be hit to release or tighten the wedges. This permits a closer clamp placement.

The bar clamps, in use, on a wood panel for a cabinet. Photographs, Courtesy, artist

When one views a finished sculpture installed, one rarely appreciates the work, power and planning behind the project. This huge 70-foot red COSMIC MAYPOLE involved four years of work for sculptress-carver Georganna Pearce Malloff and a guild of workers that evolved to assist her. The MAYPOLE, carved in the round, is differentiated from Indian totems that are carved only in a frontal area. The symbology draws on the mythology of many cultures to depict creation.

COSMIC MAYPOLE was raised in 1980 as part of the Harbourfront Sculpture Project in New Westminster, Toronto, Ontario, Canada. Photographs, Julian Bowron

M

Mel Mordaunt's shared studio in an industrial area of the Berkeley, California, waterfront has an incredible amount of space. The large stroke sander is almost diminutive compared to the scale of the studio-workshop. Photograph, Dona Meilach

Robert E. March planes a table leg. Photograph, John I. Russell

Steve Madsen's precious boxes become a reality in a portion of a huge factorylike building on the outskirts of Albuquerque, New Mexico. Space, tools and an organized workbench are important essentials to Steve for the variety of intricately designed, ambitious boxes that often make a social statement. The box below is one example. Another is on page 4. Photograph, Dona Meilach

FACTORIES IN THE FIELDS WHERE THE RIVERS USED TO FLOW. Steve Madsen. 1978. Wood, Plexiglas, silver. 24" high, 22" wide 9" deep. A box with six drawers. Courtesy, artist

John Makepeace, right, has an impressive gallery, workshop and school. It is housed in an old castle, Parnham House (BELOW), in Beaminster, Dorset, southern England. Makepeace designs one-of-a-kind furniture and several production pieces which are created by apprentices and associates. Courtesy, artist

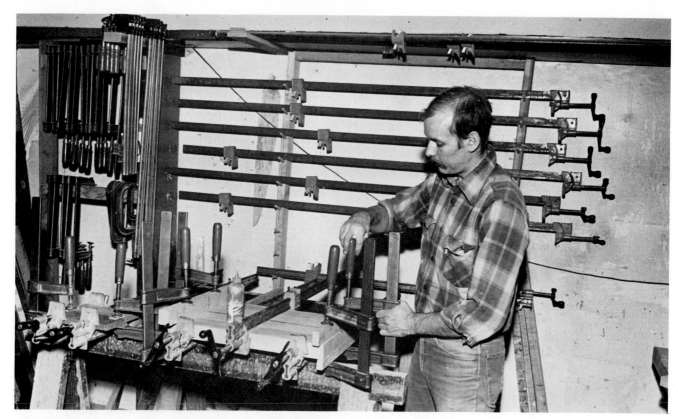

Ejner C. Pagh works at this "gluing station"—one portion of his well-equipped shop especially designed so clamps are arranged and within easy reach. Two sawhorses, approximately waist high, make it easy to set up jigs and to glue irregular shapes. One of the sawhorses has holes drilled the length of its top to accept steel rods that protrude vertically and prevent the bar clamps from tipping over when gluing things up. Ejner also uses pine cleats running perpendicular to the glue lines on the tops and bottoms of the panels to level out the various glue joints.

Another aid is the use of ¼-inch Plexiglas pads to level out joints and prevent glue from turning black and thus penetrating the wood deeply when it comes in contact with the steel clamps. Glue will not stick to the Plexiglas. Strips of paper between bar clamps and wood also keep the glue from turning black and staining the wood.

Ejner's display area (BELOW), workshop, and drying room for lumber are behind a rather drab glass-front display area. "Drab" says Ejner, "because I really do not get walk-by traffic. My display area is not 'spruced up' in the normal retail sense. Time, money and effort are spent on a quality product and not on the surrounding area. I feel the product sells itself."

The shop is located in an economically depressed downtown business area of Rockford, Illinois, but commissions come from all over, and Ejner's furniture is also on display at Mindscape Gallery, Evanston, Illinois. Courtesy, artist

ABOVE: Michael Pearce had the twelfth of a limited-production walnut dining-room table in progress in the basement workshop of his home when I interviewed him. The "deep throat" saw in the background is an antique 36-inch Orton band saw. It is amazingly vibration free and is indispensable for cutting large shapes with irregular curves. Photograph, Dona Meilach

BELOW: Saswathan Quinn's environment is a large light-flooded partitioned area in an industrial building. To support the habit he likes, creating custom-designed furniture, he also produces cube styles of furniture and custom cabinets for decorators. Photograph, Dona Meilach

Much of Frank Smullin's work results from his facility and precision use of a chain saw for blocking out, refining and achieving details. The chain saw has become a basic tool for a majority of woodworkers, each developing his own attitudes about when, where and how to evolve the shapes he wants with the tool.

Frank has acquired a variety of aids, not normally associated with woodworking, to help transport the logs that he uses for his raw materials and for manipulating in-progress and finished sculptures.

A hydraulic patient lifter, used in hospitals, is mounted on a wheeled chassis with legs that adjust to go around or under a table or stand.

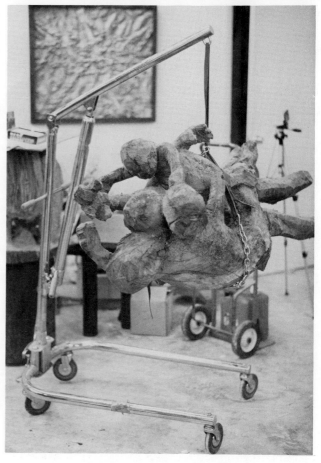

A Barrentine crop-straddling tractor, bought as United States government surplus, is used as a movable gantry for transporting logs and large sculptures up to about 1½ tons. It can straddle a form as large as a small car. He finds it indispensable for bringing logs and sculptures from the field to his studio and for a variety of other lifting and carrying jobs.

For ultimate ease in working at various heights, Frank has adapted the hydraulic base from a dental chair to raise, lower and turn a work in progress. It is heavy, stable and adjustable in height and rotates and locks in position. He says, "It is especially important in chain sawing where the work has to be placed at a height that optimizes control of the saw and gives a good shot at the work from the correct grain direction." Surplus surgical operating-table bases may also be used for this purpose, and several artists reported various improvisations with these versatile units. Photographs, artist

Barbara Spring blocks out large forms with an electric chain saw. She uses a gas-powered chain saw when she searches for wood in the countryside and along river banks. Much of the wood she uses has been gleaned from the "dead matter" of old bridges—logs, timber and other debris left to rot when bridges were changed to steel and concrete. Barbara's studio, along the California coast, was constructed with castoff materials for about $75.00. Courtesy, artist

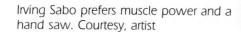

Irving Sabo prefers muscle power and a hand saw. Courtesy, artist

Dean Santner's shop is carefully laid out for maximum efficiency and it is always kept clean. Most of the machines are along the walls with only the planer, table saw and jointer in the center so that four people can work effectively to create the boxes and other objects that now have national distribution. Photograph, Dona Meilach

Bob Trotman uses a variety of hand tools for his carved and resin-inlaid boxes with faces on the covers. Photograph, Jane Trotman

Jane Teller creates huge imposing architectonic sculptures in a large, well-lit studio in New Jersey. Courtesy, artist

William Tickel, far removed from the influences of East and West coasts, creates a style that is quite unique in his Denver, Colorado, workshop, which is a high-ceilinged garage. Courtesy, artist

Sam Talarico's drying barn in Mohnton, Pennsylvania, Courtesy, artist

Ed Vega's multimedia sculptures in wood and plastic are first created as a mock-up made with cardboard and aluminum. The artist carries his command of media into another direction with lithographs that repeat the thrust of his sculptures. The lithographs are made at the Tamarind Institute, Albuquerque, New Mexico. Photographs, Dona Meilach

Woodworking: The New Wave

Robert C. Whitley's work has evolved into many styles; each turn of his creative mind has resulted in unique designs that have proven to be a major statement in contemporary furniture trends. He achieves a marvelous balance of function, tradition, avant-garde and restraint to create a harmonious statement. He avoids the faddish styles and strives for a timeliness and timelessness in his constantly evolving designs. In addition to the woodworking, he has evolved an important promotional program for his works as tasteful, restrained and effective as the objects he makes.

A design prototype for a chair in the CONTINUUM SERIES. Robert uses plywood in a prototype to help establish proper positioning and shaping of the seat back and other parts. Courtesy, artist

RIGHT: CHARIOT CHAIR—CONTINUUM SERIES. Robert C. Whitley. Curly maple, with walnut crotch pegs and mulberry and ebony centers. 36" high, 26" wide, 29" deep. Courtesy, artist

Fumio Yoshimura ponders a question during our interview in his fifth-floor New York loft studio, which looks down on the bustling city. The realism of the objects he creates, his kites, overhead, and the intricate drawings permeate the visual senses while they quietly utilize sculptural space. There is a magic in Fumio's pieces. He uses simple materials, usually a Swedish linden wood. He is humble and matter of fact about the apparent ease with which he makes his intricate drawings and creates the "ghost of the object." The unassuming quality of the artist makes the visit a monumental experience.

The drawing of a fish skull by Fumio and the beginning of its development in wood. The carved pieces are so realistic in the natural wood that they appear almost like a fragment from a real sun-bleached skull found on the desert floor. Photographs, Dona Meilach

Index

(C.S. = color section)